SOS! The Technology Guidebook
for Parents of Tweens and Teens

"In this pragmatic, empathetic, and helpful guide Sheryl Gould has distilled excellent advice from her work with thousands of parents. Once you understand your kid's tech use more clearly, including by using technology with them, you can guide and support them in building crucial skills in navigating technology. With this book in hand, you'll get along better and reduce the fighting over screen time."

- Devorah Heitner, PhD, Author of
Screenwise: Helping Kids Thrive and Survive in Their Digital World

"If you want to ditch nagging and gain tools to work through conflicts about screen time, this resource is for you! *The Technology Guidebook for Parents of Tweens and Teens* is a stunning blend of research and practical wisdom to help parents navigate technology use in their homes. It unpacks parents' common concerns and provides practical answers to keep kids safe, find more balance, and build a stronger relationship between parents and their children with them in the process."

- Michele Mitchell, Parenting Educator, Author, Speaker

"This guidebook is exactly what every parent raising tweens and teens needs. It has every detail about what to say, how to say it, and how to structure technology to set up your kids for success and avoid the daily conflict that technology often causes. The guide that we have all been waiting for has finally arrived!"

- Dr. Sheryl Ziegler, Psy.D., Clinical Psychologist
and Author of *Mommy Burnout*

"This book is an exceptional tool in the arsenal of today's parent on a complex and highly charged topic. Her practical wisdom, educational tips, and relationship-building strategies are powerful confidence boosters for parents yet surprisingly acceptable to teens. Sheryl Gould for the Win-Win!"

- **Dennis Trittin,** CFA and Author of
Parenting for the Launch and *What I Wish I Knew at 18*

"This is the guidebook parents have been waiting for! In *The Technology Guidebook for Parents of Tweens and Teens,* Sheryl Gould, tackles a complex—and often overwhelming—aspect of parenting and breaks it all down into manageable pieces. As a parenting expert (who is a parent herself), she understands the questions, concerns, and fears parents have around teens and their use of technology. Through practical advice and smart strategies, Gould equips parents to help their kids navigate the digital world. Her approach is positive and empowering, all while prioritizing the parent-teen relationship. This is a must-read for parents!"

- **Becky Baudouin,** Speaker and Author of
Enjoy Every Minute and Other Ridiculous Things We Say to Moms

"Sheryl Gould is a trusty navigator into the world of teen/tween culture and technology. She gives us an inside look at what our kids are facing and how they're thinking, so we can parent from a place of wisdom rather than fear. I so appreciate her insight and encouragement to those of us who are in the throes of monitoring screen time and social media. This book is a must for every parent's toolbox."

- **Becky Kopitzke,** Author of
*The Cranky Mom Fix: How to Get a Happier,
More Peaceful Home by Slaying the "Momster" in All of Us*

"I parented my five children (now grown) in a time when 'tech' as we know it now was just coming onto the scene. How I wish my husband and I had had this insightful and practical book to guide us! It's full of wisdom, information, and practical how-tos to initiate screentime guidelines for your family, help keep your kids safe online, and strengthen (not strain) your relationship with them in the process. I highly recommend this for parents, grandparents, and teachers—anyone whose life includes a tween or teen!"

- **Arlyn Lawrence,** Author of
Parenting for the Launch and *Prayer-Saturated Kids*

"*SOS!* is the guidebook parents need to change the way they are helping their tweens and teens manage technology. This is the first generation of kids to be Web-enabled at every juncture, and it's been challenging for parents to find the balance. I don't know a mom or dad that isn't exasperated with their teen's screentime and isn't searching for a way to reduce the tension over tech use. I love that this book doesn't solely focus on getting children off devices, but instead encourages parents to have important conversations about technology in general. We have to do more than just simply telling adolescents to put their phone down, and fortunately Sheryl gives us the tools to keep our kids safe, teach them an important life skill, and build a stronger relationship."

- **Whitney Fleming,** Author and Founder of "Playdates on Fridays"

"Technology might be the most significant battlefield we face as parents when raising children in popular culture today. Thankfully, Sheryl Gould has written this guidebook to help moms and dads proactively lead their children regarding screen use. As a mom of six, I appreciated how Sheryl walked us through setting our family tech rules around our core values. Her book also contains helpful questions, tips, tools, and resources and is a must-read for all parents of tweens and teens."

- **Amy Carney,** Author of *Parent on Purpose*

SHERYL GOULD

SOS!
THE TECHNOLOGY GUIDEBOOK FOR PARENTS OF TWEENS & TEENS

GET THE ANSWERS YOU NEED,
KEEP THEM SAFE AND
ENJOY YOUR KIDS AGAIN

NEW YORK

LONDON • NASHVILLE • MELBOURNE • VANCOUVER

SOS! The Technology Guidebook for Parents of Tweens and Teens

Get the Answers You Need, Keep Them Safe and Enjoy Your Kids Again

© 2023 Sheryl Gould

Published in New York, New York, by Morgan James Publishing. Morgan James is a trademark of Morgan James, LLC. www.MorganJamesPublishing.com

Proudly distributed by Ingram Publisher Services.

ISBN 9781636980218 paperback
ISBN 9781636980225 ebook
Library of Congress Control Number:
2022943064

Cover & Interior Design by:
Christopher Kirk
www.GFSstudio.com

Morgan James is a proud partner of Habitat for Humanity Peninsula and Greater Williamsburg. Partners in building since 2006.

Get involved today! Visit: www.morgan-james-publishing.com/giving-back

To the first generation of steadfast parents who are feeling overwhelmed navigating their kid's technology—seeking to provide balance and guidance, keep them safe, and stay connected to their hearts:

This book is for you.

TABLE OF CONTENTS

INTRODUCTION

At what age should I allow my kids to get a smartphone?

How much screen time is okay for my kid(s)?

How do I manage their usage?

What should my tech rules and limits be?

How can I keep them safe from inappropriate content and dangerous apps?

How should I feel about Fortnite?

What do I do if I find out my kid is looking at pornography?

How do I talk to them so they won't constantly argue and will cooperate with my rules?

The list of questions goes on!

If you are reading this, you know full well—the struggle is real! We are the first generation to navigate all of this technology with our kids. We have our feet in both worlds: we remember a life without technology and now we live in the digital world. No wonder we feel overwhelmed!

Whether it's smartphones, social media, the Internet, or video games, media and tech have become a huge part of our families' lives.

All of the technology with which our kids are bombarded can affect schoolwork, relationships, emotional and physical health, and concentration—just to name a few.

And if this isn't enough, here are a few statistics that confirm our fears:

- Since 2013, rates of teenage depression and suicide have skyrocketed, the same year the proportion of Americans owning a cellphone surpassed 50 percent–and the generation now known as the iGen was born.
- Up to 40 percent of children have been involved in a cyberbullying incident.[1]
- 48 percent of teens who spend more than five hours a day on electronic devices report at least one suicide-related outcome (felt very lonely and considered, planned, or attempted suicide).[2]
- 50 percent of teens report feeling addicted to their mobile devices; 78 percent check their devices at least hourly.

Today's kids are literally surrounded by technology everywhere they go. Smartphones, high speed internet, laptops, video game consoles, tablets, and the list is growing every year. (Some restaurants even have tablets with games on the table!) Even schoolwork can be done on their devices, which can make managing it all the more difficult and frustrating.

So, what do we do?!

Here's the truth: technology is here to stay whether we like it or not. We can feel angry and complain about all of the risks, dangers,

---

1   Kowalski, R. M., Giumetti, G. W., Schroeder, A. N., & Lattanner, M. R. (2014). "Bullying in the digital age: A critical review and meta-analysis of cyberbullying research among youth." *Psychological Bulletin*, 140(4), 1073

2   http://journals.sagepub.com/doi/10.1177/2167702617723376

and challenges of navigating our kids' technology, or we can be proactive. Rather than viewing technology as "the problem," we need to decide how we will respond and what we will do to live in harmony with technology.

In the midst of your fears and frustration about technology, I hope you will remember this: when all is said and done, it is your children's well-being, character, and the strong relationship that you build with them that will matter the most.

In this book, I will answer the most common questions and concerns parents have and offer practical tips and strategies you can use, as well as valuable resources to help.

I will share how to talk to your kids about their technology, and what you need to know and understand from your tween and teen's perspective about the world they live in today. I will share tips and tools to help you have an open dialogue, ask questions, and show up in ways that will build a stronger bond rather than creating power struggles and arguments. You will be guided through setting limits that work, how to keep your kids safe, and how to get them on board. Most importantly, you will learn how to have the difficult conversations and cultivate a relationship where they will come to you when something is wrong, or they have made a poor decision.

By the time you are done reading this book, my hope is you will gain reassurance, be encouraged, and be better equipped to help you guide your kid(s) and family. The insights, tools, and resources contained within this book are all aimed towards helping you find more balance, deepen your relationships, and enjoy this precious time you have left with your kid(s) while they are still at home.

Let's jump in!

CHAPTER ONE

THE 5 MOST COMMON MISTAKES WE MAKE

I f we can take a step back and all agree that technology is here to stay whether we like it or not, the question becomes, *What can we do about it?*

I want to share with you the five most common mistakes I see parents make when it comes to navigating their kids' technology. Once we get these out of the way, we will jump in and discuss what you can do to be proactive.

#1 We Make Technology the Enemy

> *"Kids today are growing up with technology, not growing into it like previous generations. This means that much of their learning, friendships, and fun happens online."* [3]

---

3   www.wellbeing.google

One of the most common concerns I hear from parents of tweens and teens is the fear and frustration regarding the negative impact social media is having on their kids and their relationships with them.

At times we've all found ourselves wanting to throw our hands up in surrender. Other times we've wanted to throw the phone or tablet out the window. Or, we are ashamed to admit we've wrestled our kids to the ground trying to grab the controller or their phone in a moment of utter desperation (mom with hand raised emoji)! We may feel like we are on the battlefield, fighting against a relentless enemy.

It doesn't have to be this way.

When media is used meaningfully and responsibly, it can enhance daily life and our relationships with our kids (yes, it can!). Teenage brothers Benjamin and Matthew Royer commented, "To stay socially relevant, kids and teens have to stay active as much as possible online. So, when parents threaten to take away their devices, they don't always realize that they could be taking away a child's social life online and in real life."[4]

Our kids' technology doesn't need to be our foe.

#2 We Overreact out of Fear

> *"When fear is in the driver's seat, ultimately,*
> *it's not going to steer you in the right direction."*
> ~Sheryl Gould

We hear all the stories: the girl in the chatroom talking to a man pretending to be a teenager, the kid being cyberbullied with horrific consequences, a teen addicted to pornography, a girl who was caught

---

4   https://www.insighttoteenculture.com/blog-posts/teens-and-technology-from-the-teen-perspective

sexting. Not to mention, we are bombarded by the latest studies on how technology is ruining our kids and affecting their brains. It makes total sense that we are fearful! However, fear fuels anxiety, and anxiety can cause us to overreact in the moment.

In my experience of working with parents, and as a parent myself, I have found that when we feel scared, powerless, or our kids aren't communicating with us, the first thing we want to do is to grab their phone, read their texts, or get overly involved in their business. Our fear and feelings of powerlessness can cause us to battle for control.

And what parent hasn't overreacted in the heat of the moment?

However, this approach doesn't work, nor does it help us to be a person with whom our kids want to talk when they have a problem. I implore you, do not default to grabbing your kid's phone, reading their texts, or getting overly involved in their business because you're scared or feeling powerless. Don't bypass having the sometimes difficult but important conversations to help your kids make good decisions, self-regulate, and stay safe in our digital world.

It's really important that we know the difference between parenting by fear and taking the necessary steps to be responsible parents and support our kids' well-being.

#3 We Don't Set Limits/Boundaries

"Boundaries are like an anchor in a storm.
We can ride the waves with greater
peace and ease rather than being tossed by fear
with every wave that comes along.
We can stand firm and relax a little.
If they happen to step over the line,
the consequences can speak for themselves."
~Sheryl Gould

When we lack boundaries, kids don't know who's in charge. I hear from moms who are walking on eggshells because their child is ruling the family and they don't know what to do.

Although kids give off the impression they'd like to be in charge, deep down they know they need help making good decisions. Even when kids argue and make it difficult, they want their parents to lead. When kids are left in charge and there's nothing to push up against, their anxiety skyrockets.

They won't always understand why they need limits/boundaries, nor will they like them, for that matter. And while we might feel like mean moms when enforcing them, our kids desperately need them.

In fact, healthy boundaries create clarity and peace in the home—keeping them safe and us sane.

Where there are no boundaries, there is confusion and chaos. When we are constantly changing our no to yes and yes to no, it's confusing for everybody. When we are clear about our expectations and the rules in our home, we don't need to hover, be so strict, or resort to controlling behavior.

#4 We Get Sucked into Power Struggles

Power struggles lead me to entertain the notion that
I'd be better off spending a weekend at the dentist
than staying home arguing with my teenager.
~Sheryl Gould

Even though we hate when our teenagers become grizzly bears and life feels like an emotional roller coaster ride, arguing and pushing the boundaries is a necessary developmental process they must go through as they inch toward adulthood. Understanding this fact can keep you from getting hooked into power struggles and unnecessary arguments.

Here are a few pointers to avoid getting hooked in a power struggle:

- Don't engage in squabbling over who's right or wrong. A teenager will rarely say, "You know what, Mom? You're right."
- If they're angry, it's okay. You don't need to defend, argue, or convince them that your decision is the right one.
- Don't take the bait. It's easy to recognize when we take the bait because we get a little nutty. We feel out of control and, in a panic, grasp to control anything.

I know it's hard to resist the juicy bait they throw out. After all, they're so good at it! I think this is one of the hardest things to avoid doing as a parent.

The next time your adolescent tries to hook you into a power struggle, allow them to express that they're upset, take a deep breath, and resist getting into the ring with them. (You're going to find it helpful when we discuss "How to Minimize the Challenges (and Arguments): Setting Limits" in Chapter 3).

#5 We Avoid Upsetting Our Kids

"If we're dependent on our teenager liking us,
we will feel like a victim most of the time."
~Sheryl Gould

One of the biggest reasons I find parents allow their kids unlimited screen-entime is they become so beaten down from arguing that they allow their kid to drive the decision around setting limits. They don't like their kids to be upset with them. Here's the truth…sometimes, your tween or teen is going to have negative feelings towards you, and most of the time, they're not going to like the word "no." Buckle up and get comfortable with it.

Here's the truth: nine times out of 10, when you set a limit with your kids or tell them no, they're not going to like it. Give them the space to be upset. You don't need to over-explain or try to convince them to feel differently. We have to be okay with them being upset and give them the limits they desperately need.

Remember that adolescence is a time when they are fighting for independence and going through many changes. Expecting them to be calm and agreeable during such a time of transition is unrealistic.

I know it can be difficult to listen to our kids when they're whining and angry. However, as annoying as it is, it's normal and healthy for your tween or teen to express when they're angry, worried, sad, or disappointed. You don't need to fix it or change how they're feeling. What they need is for you to be able to handle whatever they're feeling and hold the boundary lines for them.

CHAPTER TWO

WHAT WE NEED TO UNDERSTAND FIRST

As members of a generation that did not grow up side by side with smartphones, many parents these days struggle to understand how to operate the computer in their pocket. What is even more important to learn, however, is how technology fits into your kids' lives. Just being a parent who knows how to screenshot a snap isn't enough, you need to seek to understand how your child uses their technology, why, and what it means to them, if you are going to be able to adequately and effectively parent them through today's technological landscape.

Here are just a few of the many topics parents need to understand first if they are facilitating a healthy relationship between their kids and their tech.

#1 Understand This Is Their World

They've got smartphones, Instagram, Snapchat, YouTube, gaming, texting, social media, apps and more. Technology is a huge part of the world in which our kids live. We have to acknowledge this fact, and with that will come a greater understanding as to why our kids would like to be (if we let them) on technology 24/7.

Right at their fingertips, tweens and teens use technology to connect with friends, like posts, comment and discuss things with others, and find humor. It's how they learn, have fun, innovate, create, research topics they're interested in, study, and do school work,

Technology is also entertainment for our kids. They might be watching "Try Not to Laugh" videos, make-up or DIY tutorials, or "famous" gamers. They may also be watching educational videos about things we never had access to as kids.

This is our kids' world today. These are not bad things. What they need is our understanding and support to help them to balance, manage, and handle technology responsibly.

#2 Understand That Was Then, This Is Now

We moan and complain a lot about our kids' technology. However, I want to challenge us to look at it from our kids' perspective and help us normalize it a little bit.

When I was growing up, I would stretch the telephone cord down the hallway and into my bedroom behind closed doors. I would talk for hours, and my mom would bang on the door, telling me it was time to hang up. I'd yell back, "Give me five more minutes!" only to have her come back twenty minutes later to bang on the door again.

When we were kids, depending on your age, we watched *Happy Days, Full House*, or *Family Matters*. YouTube has replaced those after-school sitcoms we watched as kids. Gaming is the new Dungeons and Dragons or Kick the Can.

Just like we talked about our favorite TV shows with our friends, our kids watch YouTube videos, or follow Instagram and TikTok accounts, and talk about them at school. They feel the need to catch up and watch the same videos and accounts so they can be a part of the conversation with their friends.

Gaming is the latest "sport"—and our gaming kids are competitive. They want to be the best (or at least not be the first one to die) when they are playing against their friends.

And remember when we used to pass notes in class? They text or DM (direct message). Did we want our parents reading our private notes? No. They were private, between us and our friends. It's the same with our kids' texts.

#3 Understand Their Maturity Level

One of the most common questions I'm asked is, "At what age do I allow my kid(s) to get a smartphone or tablet?" When our kids feel they are ready and when we feel they are ready can be two different things. We may want to hold off, or see our kids as being too immature. They may feel like their social life will be ruined if they don't have a cell phone to text and keep up with their friends in middle school. And we hate to think about our kid being left out. This can cause pressure not only for our kids but for us as well. It is important to try and be impartial and gauge your child's maturity level while also asking some important questions to discern not only if they are ready, but if you are ready to take on the responsibility too.

According to the latest research, on average, a child gets his or her first smartphone at 10.3 years old. That same study shows that by age 12, a full 50 percent of children have social media accounts (primarily Facebook and Instagram).[5]

Not so with the Gates family. In a recent interview with *The Mirror*, Bill Gates said he didn't let any of his children get their own

---

5   https://www.inc.com/melanie-curtin/bill-gates-says-this-is-the-safest-age-to-give-a-child-a-smartphone.html

phone until they were 14 years old. That's right: His kids, at the time of the interview 20, 17, and 14, weren't allowed to have smart phones until they were high school age.

James Steyer, CEO of Common Sense Media, a nonprofit that reviews products and content for families, didn't allow his kids to get a cell phone until high school—"*after* demonstrating they can exercise restraint and understand 'the value of face-to-face communication.'"[6] Steyer noted, "No two kids are the same, and there's no magic number ... A kid's age is not as important as his or her own responsibility or maturity level."

Rather than focusing on age, ask yourself real, relevant questions concerning the emotional maturity and well-being of your child, separate from their media use. Here are some questions to ask:

- Is my child generally happy?
- Is my child self-aware and socially and emotionally mature?
- Can my child keep track of their belongings, or are they regularly losing things?
- Is my child responsible to follow through on doing their chores and homework?
- Does my child honor limits and go to bed on time?
- Is my child socially engaged with family and friends?
- Is my child putting forth effort and doing well in school?
- Is my child pursuing interests and hobbies?
- Is my child having fun and learning in their use of digital media?
- Is their behavior positive during and after watching TV, playing video games, or hanging out online?
- Does my child follow our household rules and directions?

---

6   https://www.nytimes.com/2016/07/21/technology/personaltech/whats-the-right-age-to-give-a-child-a-smartphone.html

- Does my child spend time with friends and have activities they participate in?
- Does my child exhibit the emotional maturity to know that not everything they see online is real.
- Does my child understand social cues and have self-control versus being impulsive?
- Do I have a good relationship with my child where we can talk openly about limits and usage of technology?
- Am I ready and willing to invest the energy in having these important ongoing conversations, setting limits, and keeping my kids safe?

#4 Understand Your Role in Their Relationship with Technology

Many parents see it as their responsibility to police their children's technology use. However, thinking of yourself as "the police" puts you in an adversarial relationship with your children from the start, and is more likely to make them feel stifled by your input. Try to consider yourself a "media mentor," rather than an internet cop. You should aim to help your children see screen time as a tool to connect, create, and learn. This positions you as the good guide who wants your kids to get the most out of screen time instead of presenting yourself as the bad cop who wants to take it all away.

#5 Understand *Them*

"If parents want to communicate with their teens, they should listen to them more —and enter their technological world."
~Nicole Rice, author of *Does Your Teen TALK? No, but They Text, Snap, & TikTok: 10 Subjects Every Parent Should Ask Their TEEN to Get Them TALKING More in a Digital World*

Communication is the key to having a great relationship with our kids and provides a strong foundation for them to grow and become responsible, well-adjusted adults.

Effective communication starts with listening and being open to hearing what the other person has to say. I'm confident that we've all experienced someone in our lives demanding we do something with no apparent regard for how we're feeling or what we want. If you're like me, these aren't the kinds of people I want to listen to, nor do I want to comply with their requests. It's the same with our kids.

> *"We have two ears and one mouth*
> *so that we can listen twice as much as we speak."*
> ~Epictetus

When you get your kids involved through listening and open dialogue, you are showing them that you care what they have to say; their thoughts and viewpoints matter to you. As a result, you will increase the likelihood that they will comply with the limits. Parent-driven control, on the other hand (you dominate the conversation, you don't listen, and there is no effective two-way communication taking place), tends to backfire and cause rebellion, lying, and sneaking. Here are some sample questions that invite parent-teen dialogue:

- How do you think screen time should fit into our lives—your life and our family life?
- What do you think are positive ways to spend time online, and why? (Ask them about apps, videos, or websites that they enjoy.)
- Why might it be important to find balance and have limits?
- What do you think are some of the negative effects of technology?
- How much time do you think is appropriate when it comes to homework and balancing activities?

- Do you think social media is getting in the way of doing other things—spending time with friends, exploring other interests, being physically active, schoolwork, or participating in activities?
- What are some of your favorite things to do with friends online? Face-to-face?
- Do you have friends you consider close but with whom you mostly interact online?
- With whom would you like to spend more time in person?

CHAPTER THREE

SETTING LIMITS

"As parents, one of the most important things we can do is regularly evaluate our family priorities to determine whether we are truly living life in accordance with what we say and believe to be important."

~Amy Carney

W hen it comes to setting limits with your kids around their technology, you can start by creating an open dialogue. This will help you be a parent whom your tween or teen feels like they can talk to without fear of judgment. How do you do this? Here are some tips:

- You get your kids' input when it comes to setting limits versus laying down the law.
- You ask good questions and allow them to share their thoughts, opinions, and feelings when it comes to setting limits.

- You are accepting and non-judgmental when they share their answers. Avoid criticism.

It's important to understand what the goal is when it comes to our tweens' and teens' technology. We want to instill healthy values and give them the tools they need to increase self-awareness. If they have these valuable skills in place, and understand why limits are so important, it will teach them to make wise decisions as they move towards adulthood.

There Is No One Size Fits All

In an effort to help families curb kids' technology use, groups such as the American Academy of Pediatrics (AAP) and the World Health Organization (WHO) have released recommended numerical screen limit guidelines, but the reality is that there really is no magic number that's "just right." Setting screentime limits—and helping kids moderate their own habits—is all about finding the right balance for your family's needs and lifestyle.

It's important you find what works for you and your family. Even within a family, what works for one kid may not work for another. Each family dynamic is different. Every family has a different definition of what it means to have "healthy" or positive technology habits. We also must be prepared for rules to change as our kids get older.

It's great to start with some recommended guidelines from trusted sources. But use them as a foundation from which to build your own parameters. Try different things and find what feels right for your family. Here are some examples of goals you might have for your family around technology:

- We want to use technology to learn and improve our lives.

- We want our family to have balance regarding screen time and other activities (getting outside, being with friends and family, exercise, unplugged downtime, sleep).
- We want our kids to learn to communicate in positive ways online and offline.
- We want face-to-face time with our kids/family, like having family night and fun together.

Clarify Your Beliefs

We can feel so reactive around our kids' technology that we don't pause long enough and take the time to get clear about the *what* and *why* when it comes to navigating our tweens' and teens' technology.

Here are a few questions for reflection. I encourage you to get out a piece of paper and jot down your answers.

- What are your biggest areas of concern/angst?
- What values do you want to cultivate and uphold in your family?
- What are the main reasons (your why) behind the limits and ground rules you want to set?
- What answers do you need to move forward and be proactive?

Your answers to these questions will help you define your values, set technology ground rules, and understand the positive outcomes you want.

Define Your Values with the End Goal in Mind

When we focus on setting limits, it's helpful to take an eagle's eye view. What I mean by an eagle's eye view is stepping back, reflecting on the bigger picture, and asking yourself some vital questions.

I want you to imagine for a moment the season of life when your child leaves your home—for college, the work force, and eventually a home of their own. What kind of a relationship would you like to have with your adult child?

- What values would you like to have instilled in them?
- What memories would you like them to have?
- How would you like to have prepared them as they go into the big, wide world?
- What character traits do you want to have modeled and cultivated?

Set Boundaries and Limits

Here are some questions you'll want to discuss and develop guidelines around:

- Where should devices go at night and when your children are not using them?
- Where can they go/not go online?
- What is in place to help them stay safe and private online?
- What consequences should there be if they break your online safety rules?

Here are some ideas on areas where you can set reasonable boundaries and limits:

- No phones during homework or study time (if this is a distraction for them).
- No phones at dinner.
- No phones, iPads, or computers in the bedroom after a specific time.
- No phones during family night or outings.

Focus on a Few Goals

I encourage you to identify what matters the most to you when it comes to your kids and your family. I have included space below for you to write down your goals and keep them for a reference. When it comes to "deciding what your expectations, limits, and rules will be, you can use this as a guide to help you align with what you want for your kids and your family.

What matters the most to me when it comes to my kids and family:

_____

_____

_____

_____

_____

_____

_____

_____

Be Humble

For many of us, if we're honest, our reactivity towards our kids' technology may in fact be an excellent example of "the pot calling the kettle black."

It's easy to focus on the amount of time my teen uses technology, but, if I'm honest, sometimes I am not much better. I get distracted by work deadlines, blog writing, emails, looking at Facebook, texting, and the list goes on. Rather than being so critical of my kids and the ways they are absorbed with technology, I need to own the fact that I, too, can be easily distracted by technology.

When we embrace humility, are less judgmental, and are willing to admit our own struggles with having a healthy balance between online and offline time, our kids will be more receptive to what we have to say when we discuss setting limits around our technology.

Recognize How Technology Can Also Be a Positive in Your Tween/Teen's Life

> *"Parents hold a very strong bias that 'tech is bad for teens' and fail to acknowledge ANY sort of positive factor that technology plays in modern life. Teens can be presented to be these mindless beings who haveno control over themselves whatsoever, and that technology controls them."*
> ~15-year-old teen

Many of us worry what technology is doing to our kids. And while there is no substitute for face to face communication, in-person activities and having downtime, it's important to our kids for us to remember and balance the positive aspects of what technology offers them (and us).

Here's a list from 15-year-old Louis to remind us of the positive aspects technology offers our kids:

- Studying: There are many study sources online that can help further a teen's academic ability.
- Current events: Teens can stay updated with news and events and start discussions based on what they find.
- Help: If teens feel suicidal, depressed, anxious, etc., they can turn to a hotline or quickly call a friend if they need help.

- Creativity: Artistic and musical kids can create wonders on technology and practice their skills anytime they want to.
- Safety: Letting a kid carry their phone means that they have a tool for emergency services if they ever need it.
- Curiosity: There are sites out there that let kids indulge in their curious minds and maybe even encourage them to try something new.
- School: Students use technology for almost all of their papers and projects, and it's a tool that can help them work more easily and learn from mistakes they may make.
- Happiness: Teens can find new shows or musical artists/YouTubers/blogs that encourage them to be who they are and make them laugh and smile when they desperately need it.
- Reading: Instead of spending a lot of money on hard copies of books, you can buy them cheaper on a Kindle/Kindle app and teens can enjoy reading during their downtime.
- Escape: If kids are having a bad day or need to drown out the bad things that are happening at home/in public, teens can use their devices as a way to calm themselves down (especially in abusive households).
- A general tool for aid: If you're a musician, you can download tuners and metronomes. If you're hoping to lose weight, you can follow along with exercise videos online. If you're an artist, you can look up references and tips on how to draw. If you're a baker, you can look up recipes and tips.[7]

---

7   https://www.commonsensemedia.org/movie-reviews/screenagers/user-reviews/child

Use Technology to Bond and Have Fun

You have likely heard the old adage, "If you can't beat them, join them." Along the same line, a new study out of Brigham Young University said that teens who are connected with their parents on social media feel closer to them in real life. This illustrates our need to reframe our perspective from "technology is the problem" to "technology can offer us positive opportunities to connect our kids and have fun." How do you do this? You look for creative ways to use social media that benefits your relationship with your kids. Here are a few ideas to use technology positively as a family:

- Invite them to show you their favorite YouTube or TikTok channel
- Learn something new together
- Play a video game together
- Find an online recipe and make a meal together
- Make Pinterest boards for topics you are both interested in
- Make a music video
- Visit a virtual museum or vacation destination
- Use funny face apps to snap pictures or trade faces
- Look up a tutorial to learn how to do something new
- Look up funny apps and take turns sharing your creative finds
- Learn some new on TikTok or do a dance together
- Try a virtual yoga or exercise class
- Explore a national park
- Have a Karaoke night
- Take a coding class or learn a new language together
- Find a few YouTubers you can both enjoy following
- Follow each other on Instagram
- FaceTime a faraway relative
- Use digital wristbands to encourage everyone to be active

- Find an app to express creativity with photos, music, coloring, making funny voices, or creating your own movies
- Find and listen to a podcast that you both enjoy

Believe in Your Kids' Ability to Make Good Decisions

*"I wish they would understand that technology is not
all bad and to totally cut it out is not the solution.
I wish they would give us a little more freedom
and trust us more/give us a chance."*
~High School Student[8]

*"My parents used to go through my iPad and delete everything,
and it gave me the idea that I cannot have any sort of privacy
or personal collection of my interests. If anything, their
restrictions of demanding to look through everything makes me
not want to show them anything, or tell them anything."*
~15-year-old teen

It's important to reflect on the messages we're sending our kids when it comes to our approach towards them and technology. Are we conveying we don't trust them, even when they've proven to be trustworthy? Are we reacting out of fear, trying to control them and clamping down in a way that is hurting our relationship with them and their willingness to open up? Are we grasping for control versus having the important conversations that we need to be having? And, if they are breaking

---

8   https://protectyoungeyes.com/what-teens-wish-their-parents-understood-about-technology/

the rules, are we curious as to why that might be? Do we get their input and talk about how they can win back trust?

When it comes to your kid's technology, remember to convey the message, "I believe that you have that wisdom inside of you to make good decisions. I trust you to do that." When you believe in your kids' ability to make good decisions, this may be one of the greatest motivations for them to do just that.

Use a Contract

> *"What we need to do is empower our kids to make good decisions with this new gadget—to help them understand that a cell phone, like all privileges, is a responsibility."*
> ~Josh Shipp

Whenever your child has the privilege of using a device, it should also come with an accompanying agreement—a contract. Kids need boundaries and to know what expectations and rules are.

> *"If you're going to do a contract you need to come up with the rules with your child. It's not fair to not make a contract without your child, ESPECIALLY if you don't know anything about technology."*
> ~13-year-old boy

Contracts work best particularly when your child has a say in the terms of the contract versus having the rules imposed upon him/her. In the Resources section at the end of this book, you will find our Moms

---

9   https://www.commonsensemedia.org/movie-reviews/screenagers/user-reviews/child?page=1

of Tweens and Teens Cell Phone Contract that you can use as a guide and modify as needed to start the conversation. A cell phone contract helps you be clear about what the guidelines are in order to set limits and keep your child safe.

Whether you have a tween or teen, you can use this contract to encourage a discussion around expectations and limitations on cell phone and social media usage. Page one is suitable for all ages. For an older child, you may decide to use page two as well, which covers sexting and pornography on the web. **As we were told by an officer we interviewed, we should never assume our kids don't know something, or that one of their friends won't expose them.**

CHAPTER FOUR

ESTABLISHING GROUND RULES

"I'll see your toddler tantrum and raise you
a teen who just had their phone taken away."
~ Mommy Needs A Life

O ne of the hardest things about parenting tweens and teens and trying to navigate their technology is dealing with the fighting, the push back, and the power struggles. We are trying to be good parents who do what's right, who keep our kids safe, and who enforce limits—all while feeling like we're swimming against the current. It's a continuous, exhausting daily battle that is constantly changing.

Important Questions for Getting on the Same Page

It's best if you can discuss these things with your child and come to an agreement on them before giving him or her a phone. But, if you're playing catch up, it's not too late. You can explain to them that you've realized you neglected to communicate with them about expectations, and let them know you want everyone in the family to have clarity on what the ground rules are.

Here are some questions to ask yourself and your spouse/partner, and then discuss with your kids:

- Who's going to pay for the cell phone? What are you willing to pay for?
- Is it okay for your tween or teen to have the phone in the area where they study?
- Will you allow the phone in the bedroom? How about when they're supposed to be sleeping?
- Is it okay or not okay for them to use the phone and social media to connect with friends when they first wake up?
- Can your tween or teen use social media before they go to bed? When do you expect them to turn it off?
- Is it okay to check your child's phone without asking or should you tell them you are going to check it?

Use Your Values to Define Your Ground Rules

I encourage you to identify the values you hold dear. What are the values you'd like to model, cultivate, and uphold in your family? Reflect on how these apply when it comes to setting limits, rules, and agreements. Here are a few examples of what this might look like:

Value: *Making time for face-to-face connection and downtime*

Ground Rule: *Phone-free zones*

Enforce certain days/times when your children must put their phones down for a few hours (this means Mom and Dad too!). Movie night, trips to Starbucks, shopping, baking, family dinners, and studying can and should be done without a phone in hand. While you may hear some initial complaining, these "phone breaks" are a great way to show your teens that they can survive without their phone or social media.

Value: *Getting good sleep*

Ground Rule: *Phone off at 10:00 p.m.*

A major cause of teenage depression is lack of sleep and a big reason for this is smartphones. Not only does the light cause our kids' brains to stay awake, but many studies suggest scrolling social media before bed can increase anxiety and depressive thoughts.

Have your teen charge their phone in a room other than their bedroom. In extreme circumstances, shut the home wifi off at a specific, predetermined time.

Value: *Safety*

Ground Rule: *Have the agreement with you tween or teen that you always have your login username and password.*

Many parents struggle with the moral issue of spying on their kids, which is why I suggest not doing it. (Check out the article in the Resource Section: "Should I Read My Kids' Texts?") However, possessing the log-in username and password is the same as wearing a seat belt in an automobile. Just like the seat belt is a layer of protection from an automobile crash, your ability to access their social media, if necessary, protects tweens and teens online.

Value: *Productivity*

Ground Rule: *Screen time will not take away from needed productivity time—e.g., schoolwork, chores, reading, college applications, clubs and activities, etc.—things that contribute to being an educated and well-rounded person.*

The older our kids get, the more important their time is, and the need to use it wisely and appreciate the opportunity costs of having screens dominate their lives. Much of their tech time is really recreational/social/entertaining rather than productive, which can contribute to distraction, lack of attention, lack of self-discipline, laziness, and a reduced commitment to being well-rounded, creative, and knowledgeable. It can also distort the work/play division that was much more obvious for past generations; many people (of all ages, not just tweens and teens) fail to recognize that tech use is causing a much larger play component in their lives. This has the potential to severely impact productivity and, some might say, to actually "dumb down" our kids and society.

With some of these very values in mind, here are some of the school year screen time rules moms shared in our Moms of Tweens and Teens community:

"No phones at the dinner table for EVERYONE! They give me their phones to charge at night. No phone in rooms at night on a school night and everything shuts down at 9:00 p.m." - Trisha H.

"One hour a day after homework. Any more than that has to be earned through chores, helping when not expected to, doing homework without fighting etc. these can all earn time (15 to 30 minutes, depending on what he did)." - Harmony W.

"No electronics (phones, Xbox, Switch) past 8:00 p.m. on school nights for my 12-year-old. But otherwise no limit on anything else. Or weekends. Be respectful. Do as I ask. Get up for school and you must play a sport. Be a good kid and there are no limits on anything." - Emily K.

"30 minutes when she gets home from school then it's mine until homework, studying, and chores are complete. 9:00 p.m. phone curfew."- Paula L.

"No screen time after 10:00 p.m. for my kids, including my 10th grade son. He pretty much hates me, but oh well!"- Jenni L.

"Chores and all schoolwork must be completed before she touches her iPad. I make a list of chores for the week and she's responsible for them. If she does what she is supposed to do she can have four hours." - Elle D.

"No Xbox during the week, five hours on Saturday, Sunday, three hours on Friday." - Barbara B.

"We have a deal with ours. As long as they get themselves up on time for school every day/ get themselves ready/ they do good in school and keep up with everything we ask of them (school/ keeping bedrooms clean/ clean up after themselves/ take care of their personal belongings), there is no bedtime or limitations on the internet. We have been doing it for a few years now. And, surprisingly it works out great." - Brittany V.

Enlist Their Cooperation

It's helpful, when it comes to encouraging cooperation, to include your tween or teen in setting the limits and coming up with consequences. But first, you need to identify the problem and talk about it.

This isn't always easy to know how to do.

Sometimes a great way to do this is to identify a problem—for example, your son is playing Fortnite and when you tell him to get off, he doesn't. You find your frustration rising: you wind up yelling and a full-blown argument ensues.

What can you do instead? Use this script below. I find this to be an effective approach when it comes to setting limits and minimizing conflict while encouraging cooperation. (Note: You want to pick a good time to have this discussion.)

You: *"I'm noticing* _____(express the problem). *I'm noticing you're on Fortnite for over four hours a day. When I tell you it's time to get off, you don't listen, and you tell me you'll get off in five minutes. I wind up yelling and it turns into an argument."*

You: Say what you don't want, and share feelings. *"I don't want to keep nagging and yelling. And it doesn't feel good when I keep reminding you and you're not listening. And I'm imagining it doesn't feel good to you either."*

You: Say what you want. *"I want us to come up with a strategy or agreement as to how we can handle this so we're not arguing about this constantly. I don't like it and I know you don't either. I have some thoughts and I'd like to hear what you think."*

You: Share your thoughts and talk about what you can do to come to an agreement.

If possible, together come up with a consequence if the limit or agreement isn't followed.

Let your tween or teen know the consequences they can expect and make sure to follow through (more on that in the next chapter). Check back in after a few days or a week to debrief and talk about what is working or not working.

When They Protest

Expect that when you set limits and/or decide to use parental controls, they won't like it, at least at first. They will whine, protest, ask why 10 to 20 times, and be upset when they run out of time.

Remind yourself why you are setting limits:

- You are training them in time management, to self-regulate, and to follow through with their responsibilities.
- You are supporting them to embrace other activities (such as clubs, exercise, working, spending face-to-face time with their friends, smelling the roses, or cleaning their rooms).

Be encouraged that, after a little time, it will be the new normal:

- The questions will stop, things will go well, and you will feel as though you can reward them with extra time sometimes.
- With parental controls in place, it will start to run itself as if you have no involvement at all.

Provide Positive Incentives

We can use technology to teach our kids so many important life skills: time management, exercising self-control, strengthening their problem-solving skills, and increasing self-awareness.

Our kids' technology can be a strong motivator for getting their homework or chores completed and reinforcing their positive choices.

For example, if your son sets a timer and gets off his video game without you asking, then he gets a half an hour extra time over the weekend. If your daughter puts her cell phone in your room on the charger without you reminding her, she gets to pick the restaurant you go to on Friday night. Incentives acknowledge and affirm our kids for the positive choices they're making and motivate them to keep it up.

Establish Consequences

When you've clearly communicated the limits and boundaries have been broken, you need to hold your tween or teen accountable by following through with the consequence. Here are some suggestions to help you establish this framework in your own household:

1. **Emphasize follow through versus lecture.** It's important that your tween or teen understand the expectations and limits that you set. Include them in the process; allow them to have their say and make sure to listen. Be clear what the consequence will be and, when they don't adhere to the limit or boundary, follow through. Here's an example that might help:

   Let's say you set a limit for your son that he can play one hour on his video game after homework is done on a school night and after chores are done—only to find out that he hasn't done his chores. A consequence might be that he loses the video game for the rest of the evening, or he loses that hour the next day or over the weekend.

2. **Understand they will make mistakes and push the boundaries.** Simply put, this is their job—to test the limits at this age. Instead of wasting your energy getting angry, pat yourself on the back for setting limits that they can push up against. This is how they feel safe.

3. **Don't expect them to like having consequences.** Chances are they will whine and complain. Expect it. Do you enjoy suffering a consequence, such as running out of gas when you forget to fill the tank? Same thing. This is how they learn, and it's uncomfortable.

4. **Hold the line.** The biggest yellers and complainers are those who have no boundaries. There is no need to yell when you

follow through with a consequence. The consequence does the work for you. When you follow through and hold your tween or teen accountable, you will be taken seriously. They will learn that there are consequences for their choices, either positive or negative. Remind yourself that they had a choice and you're holding them accountable.

5. **Admit when you make mistakes.** Our kids are really percep-tive at sensing our inconsistencies in our expectations towards them and our behaviors. Of course, age plays a role in our technology use. However, if you tell your tween or teen that you're not going to do something (or you are going to do something), and you don't do what you say, avoid getting defensive when they point it out. Rather than being defen-sive, admit your mistake and apologize. It's amazing the dif-ference it makes in our kids' willingness to own their mistakes when we can admit our own.

Encourage Positive Online Behavior

On a regular basis, people share with me how they're having a conflict with someone over a text or email that's gotten out of hand. I encour-age them to reach out, pick up the phone, or have a face-to-face con-versation where they can actually hear the tone of voice and the heart of what the other person is saying. One of the downsides of technology is it can dull our senses to how our words and behaviors impact others.

Our tweens and teens are especially susceptible to not understand-ing how their words and actions online, or through text, impact other people. And, all of these exchanges come at a time when their brains are undergoing reconstruction; they lack impulse control and can be quick to respond without thinking.

It's important to encourage and discuss positive online behavior and what's appropriate and what's not.

Here are a few areas to discuss:

- Commenting on social media about personal issues is not really appropriate. Discuss the importance of not saying anything they wouldn't say to someone's face.
- When responding back to someone when they're upset, encourage them to pause. When they do respond, recommend they ask themselves if their comment is kind, constructive, and respectful. If they answer "no" to any of these three questions, then they should take a time out to think through their response.
- Talk about the importance of respecting other points of view and beliefs.
- Talk about treating people online with the same respect you would give them face-to-face.
- Discuss the importance of reporting bullying behavior to you directly instead of engaging with it.

It's important for your tween or teen to understand how mobile technology can affect their future. Share with them that their online reputation is important. Businesses and colleges are spending time searching social media when they are looking at applicants. Ask them to think about what messages they might be sending and if that is how they really want others to see them.

CHAPTER FIVE

KEEPING THEM SAFE

"Constant access to digital devices lets kids escape uncomfortable emotions like boredom, loneliness, or sadness by immersing themselves in video games or social media. We're now seeing the effects of what happens when a generation spends their childhood avoiding discomfort. Electronics are replacing opportunities to develop mental strength and gain the coping skills they need to handle everyday challenges."

~Amy Morin

O ur kids may feel isolated, sad, or lonely and turn to social media to feel better. For other kids, social media may reinforce feelings of sadness, not quite fitting in, or the pressure to look or be a certain way.

Here are some things to be on the lookout for in this department:

#1 CyberBullying

"I am a huge advocate for anti-bullying in our youth.
What I have seen with the rise of social media is
that children are not facing bullying on a playground,
they are facing it on their cell phones."
~Whitney Wolfe Herd

The definition of cyberbullying is "the spreading of embarrassing, humiliating, harassing, or damaging communication via the internet or via cell phones by text or picture messages." The effects of cyberbullying can have devastating consequences. And it's especially difficult for our kids to get away from it.

Cyberbullying can result in a child who faces the struggle of anxiety, emotional pain and trauma, low self-esteem, skipping school, damaged friendships, depression, and—in rare cases—suicide. As parents, we need to be aware that cyberbullying may be happening in our homes without us even knowing it. We must do our best to protect and talk to our kids.

What you can do if you find out your tween or teen is being bullied:

- Take threats seriously, even if your child says, "They are joking." Others may not know it's a joke.
- Don't minimize the bullying or tell your child to ignore or get over it. The emotional pain of being bullied is very real and can have long-lasting effects.
- Be supportive and understanding.
- Find out how long the bullying has been going on and assure your child that you'll work together to find a solution. Let your children know they are not to blame for being bullied.

- Do not retaliate— this only allows the bully to justify his behavior and the victim is seen as contributing to the problem.
- Tell them not to respond to any cyberbullying threats or comments online.
- Don't delete. Instead, print out all the messages, take screenshots, note online screen names, email addresses, and any other information available to you. You will need the messages to verify and prove there is cyberbullying.
- Don't threaten to take away the child's computer or cell phone if they come to you and share a problem. This can lead to them being more secretive.
- Talk to your school's guidance counselors so they can keep an eye out for bullying during the school day.
- Get law enforcement involved if there are threats of physical violence or bullying that continues to escalate.

And, perhaps most importantly, let them know that it's important to you that they know that when they are struggling with anything to reach out for guidance and support or just to talk about it. Encourage them, of course, to come to you, but also to make sure not to remain alone in their pain—to talk to a trusted friend, social worker, or teacher at school, or even a family member they feel comfortable with, no matter what.

Additional resources on cyberbullying are in the resource section at the back of the book.

#2 Body Image and the Obsession to Look Perfect

"There's an obsession to portray a picture perfect version of your life—so much so that we've forgotten that each one of us has

flaws, the kind that make us imperfectly perfect.
We are human. Not robots."[10]

~Jennifer, a High School Senior / Quoted from the *Selfless* Movie
Documentary

"Children used to get bullied at school. Now they go home, and
that's where the problem starts. because they sit on their phones
all night, thinking about who's 'liked' a photo of them, who hates
them, who loves them. They don't know what's real and what's
not, editing their lives constantly to fit other people's views."[11]

~Jessie J.

The obsession to look perfect has become increasingly common among tweens and teens in recent years.

When I was growing up, I saw the popular girl down the hall at school. I envied her hair, her clothes, and how thin and pretty I thought she was. Then, I went home for the day (or weekend) and put her out of my mind.

Now our kids have Instagram, Snapchat, Tik Tok, and YouTube. They are bombarded on a

daily basis every time they open their phones with unrealistic expectations. They follow teen influencers and celebrities that curate their images, never take a bad picture, wear the latest fashions, and have idealized, perfect-sized bodies. Back in the day, we had magazines that we purchased at the store. Today, it's hard for them to get away from the staged and filtered pictures that make people look like they've got it all

---

10   https://freshindependence.com/
11   http://www.morefamousquotes.com/topics/quotes-about-phones-in-school/

together. It's easy to see why they could feel like their appearance never measures up to what society deems worthy of attention and approval.

And the pressure to look a certain way doesn't just impact our girls. Boys definitely feel the pressure as well, with an increase in studies being done on the impacts of muscular and lean body types being idealized.

This unrealistic, fictitious perfect image can lead to low self-esteem, depression, eating disorders, discontent, anxiety, and even suicidal thoughts.

Our kids need our help sorting through the false messages and beliefs they receive constantly from daily exposure to social media. These continually messages of "not good enough" and feeling less then can cause long-term emotional baggage.

Here are some questions or topics for conversation aimed to help our children understand the individual impact these "ideal" images may be having on them:

- "I know that there can be a lot of pressure to look a certain way on Instagram, being a certain weight or having the perfect muscular body, or capturing the perfect image in order to get a certain number of likes. Do you sometimes feel that way?"
- "How do you notice you feel after scrolling through Instagram? Do you notice you feel more critical of yourself after being on social media?"
- Affirm with your kids that we all long for attention, approval, and acceptance, and that social media can make people appear to look even "better" than they do in real life.
- Discuss the power of examining accounts that they follow, how these accounts make them feel, and the internal messages that we all can take in without even being aware of it.

- Talk about the importance of being conscious and noticing, when we see certain images, the critical voices we may be developing in our heads. You can even ask them what messages they notice they are telling themselves.

- Talk about what might be some accounts they may need to unfollow, ones that increase the feelings of "not good enough," and how they can be more proactive to follow accounts that have encouraging and positive messages that make them feel good about themselves. (Note: one of the most important ways you can support your kids to feel confident and good about their bodies is to feel better about yourself and build your *own* body confidence!)

- Discuss your body in a positive way and be careful when you are tempted to say things like, "My thighs look fat," or, "I hate my hair." Catch yourself and instead say something affirming and kind to yourself.

- Focus on character, valuing who you and your child uniquely are created to be, and living a meaningful and purposeful life versus focusing on appearance.

In the Resources section of this book, you will find videos you can use to spark conversations about the messages that social media is sending to our daughters and sons.

> *"There's so much more to life than trying to shrink, than constantly comparing your body, your life, to someone else's. Than trying to be something other than exactly who you were meant to be. It's time to stop living small, babe . . .*
> *you were made for so much more!"*
> ~Allison Kimmey, Body Positivity Instagrammer

#3 FOMO (The Fear of Missing Out)

"Teenagers spoke about the pressure they felt to make themselves available 24/7, and the resulting anxiety if they did not respond immediately to texts or posts. Teens are so emotionally invested in social media that a fifth of secondary school pupils will wake up at night and log on, just to make sure they don't miss out."[12]

YouTube, Instagram and Snapchat are the most popular online platforms among teens. Fully 95 percent of teens have access to a smartphone, and 45 percent say they are online "almost constantly." They may check Instagram, Snapchat, or TikTok dozens (or more!) times a day. While this is how many tweens and teens connect with their friends, it can also leave them feeling stressed out, irritable, and exhausted.

This social media-specific anxiety has a name: FOMO, also known as "fear of missing out."

FOMO comes in many forms:

- They feel the stress to constantly keep up. If they don't respond right away, they may worry that a friend will be mad at them.
- If they're in a text chain and don't answer, they may think they will be excluded from the group or miss out on a conversation.
- They see friends post pictures of getting together and wonder why they weren't invited.
- There is something constantly happening all the time, and if they're not online too, then they will miss out. They want to belong and fit in at this age, and it's overwhelming for them to try to keep up with it all.

---

12 https://www.theguardian.com/commentisfree/2015/sep/16/social-media-mental-health-teenagers-government-pshe-lessons

Parents can help. If you see your kids struggling—maybe they're always stressed out after being on the phone or they're staying up too late texting—step in. Here are some things you can do:

- **Don't judge. Listen instead.** While this can drive us crazy and stress us out when we see our kids obsessed with their phones, remember that this is their social life. It's easy to judge and identify these forms of connection today as being "bad." Remember, at this age it is so important to them that they feel like they "belong." They want to fit in. So the more you can understand, listen, and empathize, the more they will open up and talk to you when they're feeling stressed out.

- **Encourage their offline lives.** Encourage them to find activities that build them up and cultivate confidence and a strong sense of who they are and what makes them unique and feel good about themselves. Have them pick one activity each semester—a club, sports, drama or music, a job, volunteering, etc.

- **Encourage them to seek out real connections.** Encourage them to make plans with a friend, organize a group activity, or do anything social that connects them face to face with others.

- **Don't be afraid to set limits** on the amount of time they spend on their phone.

- **Ask questions** and listen without judgment (some sample conversation starters are on page 80)

#4 The Comparison Game and Low Self-Esteem

"In my pursuit of happiness, I began taking bikini pictures and selfies. I felt my confidence was restored and reassured temporarily

by a click of a button. But now, I was trapped too."[13]
~Jennifer, from the documentary Selfless

"Teens who have created idealized online personas may feel frustrated and depressed by the gap between who they pretend to be online and who they truly are. They compare themselves and the number of likes they receive."[14]

Social media makes it easy to fall into the comparison trap and feel like you're not good enough on a daily basis. Many moms have even expressed to me the pressure they feel on social media and how they compare themselves to other moms and women who appear to be doing "it" so much better than them. Sharing our own struggles in this area can be a way into starting a conversation about the pressures we can all feel.

Don't:

- Underestimate the role social media plays in the lives of teenagers
- Dismiss or minimize your tween or teen's experiences. For them, things like the number of likes, negative comments, break-ups, or being left out brings up feelings that are very real to them.

Do:

- Encourage them to think about social media in a more critical way. Some of the questions below can help you to have these conversations.

---

13   https://freshindependence.com/
14   https://childmind.org/article/social-media-and-self-doubt/

Questions to Discuss with Them:

- How does social media make you feel?
- What do you like? What don't you like?
- Do you think your friends are really the people they appear to be online?
- How do you want people to perceive you on social media? Why?
- What do you think are some of the downsides of social media?
- What makes a good photo?
- What is it about getting "likes" that feels good?
- How does posting and looking at social media affect your mood?
- What apps do you like best?
- What would happen if you turned off your phone for an hour (or two) a day? How might you feel?
- What are the pros and cons of using Instagram, Snapchat, and other social networking apps?
- What would happen if you unfollowed or unfriended someone who was making you feel bad on social media?

Providing perspective can help. Discuss how these images show the best part of people's lives and you don't see what's really going on underneath the surface—the homework struggles, feelings of anxiety or inferiority, the fight they just had with their parents, or even how many times they had to take the picture to make it look as good as possible so they could get more likes.

Teens and tweens (and even us) need to be reminded that social media isn't an accurate representation of someone's life. Remind them that social media leaves the messy stuff out—and that everyone has struggles and challenges that we may not be aware of.

#5 Increased Anxiety and Depression

"We're training and conditioning a whole new generation of people that when we are uncomfortable or lonely or uncertain or afraid we have a digital pacifier for ourselves that is kind of atrophying our own ability to deal with that."
~Tristan Harris, Former Design Ethicist at Google and Co-founder of Centre for Humane Technologies

Is using social media making our kids unhappy? Evidence is mounting that there is a link between social media and depression. In several recent studies, teenage and young adult users who spend the most time on Instagram, Facebook, and other platforms were shown to have a substantially (from 13 to 66 percent) higher rate of reported depression than those who spent the least time.[15]

A survey conducted by the Royal Society for Public Health[16] asked 14 to 24-year-olds in the UK how social media platforms impacted their health and well-being. The survey results found that Snapchat, Facebook, Twitter, and Instagram all led to increased feelings of depression, anxiety, poor body image, and loneliness.[17]

Does that mean that Instagram and Facebook are actually *causing* depression? These studies show a correlation, not causation. But it's worth a serious look at how social media could be affecting teenagers and young adults negatively. One reason the correlation seems more than coincidental is that an increase in depression occurred in tandem with the rise in smartphone use.

---

15   https://childmind.org/article/is-social-media-use-causing-depression/
16   https://www.rsph.org.uk/our-work/campaigns/status-of-mind.html
17   https://www.theguardian.com/commentisfree/2015/sep/16/social-media-mental-health-teenagers-government-pshe-lessons

A 2017 study of over half a million eighth through twelfth graders found that the number exhibiting high levels of depressive symptoms increased by 33 percent between 2010 and 2015. In the same period, the suicide rate for girls in that age group increased by 65 percent.[18] Smartphones were introduced in 2007, and by 2015 fully 92 percent of teens and young adults owned a smartphone. The rise in depressive symptoms correlates with smartphone adoption during that period, even when matched year by year, observes the study's lead author, San Diego State University psychologist Jean Twenge. Over that same time period, there was a sharp spike in reports of students seeking help at college and university counseling centers, principally for depression and anxiety. Visits jumped 30 percent between 2010 and 2015.[19]

So, the question becomes: what do we do about it?

- Focus on building a healthy relationship with your kids. Listen to what they have to say. Be a safe place for them to open up without fear of judgement, criticism, or giving unsolicited advice.
- Label feelings and share them. Even the negative ones. Encourage a culture in your home where everyone feels safe to share their feelings and what is weighing on their heart. Depression and anxiety grow bigger and feel more unbearable and overwhelming when we are isolated or feel alone in our pain. Model sharing your feelings and where you are at in the moment, such as, "I'm feeling stressed out about my work deadline," or, "I'm feeling frustrated right now about the mess in the kitchen. I need everyone to help out," or, "I'm excited to see your grandma. I've missed her," or, "I was sad to hear

18   https://childmind.org/article/is-social-media-use-causing-depression/
19   https://childmind.org/article/is-social-media-use-causing-depression/

that the neighbor, Mrs. Caplan, is in the hospital." You don't want to overload your kids in such a way that they feel burdened to caretake you or help you to feel better. Instead, the goal is to label feelings. Model expressing those feelings and, as a result, inviting them to share their own feelings rather than holding them in.

- Set limits on the amount of time they are on their screens and don't rush into giving them access to Instagram just because you are feeling pressured. Make sure they are participating fully in life and have plenty of face-to-face interactions. And, when you feel they are ready, make sure you are talking to them.

- Make sure they are getting physical activity, which creates endorphins and makes them feel good about themselves.

- Encourage them to find activities they enjoy that can build confidence, a sense of accomplishment, and community.

- Spend time with them. Have fun. Find those things that they enjoy doing with you.

- Let them know you are far from perfect and that if they are struggling with anxiety or feeling down or depressed, they can come to you. Let them know that you are there for them no matter what, and nothing they do or say would ever cause you to love them any less or love them anymore.

- It's important to know the warning signs for suicide in order to spot them. Keep a close eye on an adolescent who is depressed, anxious, or withdrawn. And keep the lines of communication open. Let them know you are a safe place by expressing your care, support, concern, and love.

- If you suspect your teen might be thinking about suicide, talk to him or her immediately. Don't be afraid to use the word "suicide." Talking about suicide won't plant ideas in your teen's head. Ask your teen to talk about his or her feelings and listen. Don't dismiss his or her problems. Instead, reassure your teen of your love. Remind your teen that he or she can work through whatever is going on— and you're willing to help.

How Do You Know if You Should Be Concerned?

If you see any cause for concern, including mood swings that seem to result from social media, a lack of pleasure in activities he or she used to enjoy, and having accompanying symptoms such as headaches and stomachaches, visit your child's pediatrician for a professional opinion.

Here are the most common symptoms of a social media anxiety disorder:

- Interrupting conversations to check your social media accounts
- Lying to others about how much time you spend on social media, gaming, and YouTube
- Withdrawal from friends and family
- Trying to stop or reduce your use of media more than once before without being successful
- Loss of interest in other activities
- Neglecting work or school to comment on social media or watch a YouTube video
- Experiencing withdrawal symptoms when you are not able to access social media or video games
- Spending over six hours per day on social networking sites like Facebook, Twitter, Instagram or YouTube, and video games
- An overwhelming need to share things with others on social media sites
- Having your phone with you 24 hours a day to check your social media sites or watch YouTube
- Using social media more often than you planned

- Severe nervousness or anxiety when you are not able to check your notifications
- Negative impacts in your personal or professional life due to social media usage

I often hate to talk about the negative impacts of social media because I know how prone we are as parents to panic (I'm raising my hand). When it comes to dealing with the negative influences of social media on our kids' mental, social, and emotional health, our kids need limits. They need for us to be available and provide a safe place for them to open up and talk to us without fear of us over-reacting, judging them, or grabbing their phone.

When our own anxiety takes over, we can react quickly without reflecting and taking the time to really get to know and understand what's going on in their inner and outer worlds, which are rapidly changing and shifting and often subject to confusion.

What Are Your Child's Stressors? Do You Know?

When your child seems irritable or overwhelmed, be curious about what might be going on underneath the surface and what they might be needing. Look for opportunities where they are more prone to open up and talk—car drives, playing a video game, a trip to Starbucks, and even late at night when all you want to do is go to bed. Ask them how they're feeling and be a listening ear.

I love the 80 percent / 20 percent rule: listen 80 percent of the time and talk 20 percent. It's a great recipe for increasing the chances they will feel safe to talk to you when they are feeling or experiencing anxiety, sadness, loneliness, discouragement, depression, bullying, or the pressure to look or be a certain way.

CHAPTER SIX

UNDERSTANDING THE RISKS

"On its own, social media is not dangerous,
it's the manner in which it's used that can be the problem."
~Lori Getz, *The Tech Savvy User's Guide to the Digital World*

Devorah Heitner, digital citizen expert and author of *Screenwise: Helping Kids Thrive (and Survive) in Their Digital World*, says it well when it comes to helping our kids navigate the risks of social media:

> *"Mentor over monitor. Our kids need us to help them repair when they mess up. They may need our input when they text something funny to the group chat and other kids find it insensitive...or our guidance on how to apologize and move forward in the relationship. Monitoring can cut us off from those teaching opportunities. Maybe you don't know how to approach a conversation because you're not supposed*

> *to know about the meme your kid sent, or your kids start getting defensive about their privacy and try to get sneaky with the tech."*[20]

Isn't that the truth . . .

Our kids need us to keep them safe from the risks and dangers of social media. And, in order to be effective in keeping them safe, we actually need to educate and mentor more than monitor.

Why?

The best way to ensure your kids are safe is to keep communication open and mentor them on how to use social media responsibly and how to be discerning, kind, and wise digital citizens. Teenagers want more privacy and if you are constantly over-monitoring it can actually get in the way of opportunities to have the important conversations around safety. Over-monitoring can lead to kids sneaking around, finding ways to get around parental controls, and rebellious behavior.

I have found the challenge working with moms is we often don't know how to have these important conversations and actually come alongside our kids versus fighting against them. In this section, I'm going to share with you the dos and don'ts to protect your kids from the dangers of social media.

Keeping Them Safe

The Cell Phone Contract at the end of this book will assist you in talking through some of these points I'm going to share here. However, I'm going to exchange the risk of being repetitive for the benefit of being thorough in addressing the issue of keeping your kids safe. Here

---

20   https://www.facebook.com/RaisingDigitalNatives/
     posts/4418931798139421

are some ideas for keeping your kids safe online: (Note: These guide-lines will change as they get older.)

#1 Do:

- Keep the computer in a common area of the home.
- If your child does have a computer/device in his or her room, make a family rule that it is never used behind a closed door (i.e., if the computer/device is being used, the bedroom door is open)
- Restrict incoming communication with the use of software or programs designed to filter out inappropriate content or predators
- Talk regularly and specifically with them about online dangers (e.g., cyberbullying, pornography, predators, social media addiction/anxiety, etc.)
- Understand that filtering software isn't always perfect. Our kids can be savvy in getting around the filtering programs we use.
- Remind them that they can come to you for help if anything is inappropriate, upsetting, or dangerous, without fear of punishment.

#2 Don't:

- Threaten and immediately take the phone away. And don't over-react. If they're afraid of being punished, they will tend to not tell you. What they need is your support and guidance. Instead, talk to your kids about how important it is to:
  - Ignore communication from people they don't know.
  - Report cyber-bullying, threats, or other questionable behavior.

- Do not pass along pictures or messages that may be hurtful to another child.
- Promote "netiquette"—polite, respectful behavior online.
- When needed, ask for help from an adult.

#3 Keep Private

They need to know:

- Never give out private information if a stranger could obtain that content.
- People aren't always who they say they are. Even someone you meet on social media and chat with for months might be lying about their identity.
- Don't post your location publicly.

#4 Be Aware of Dangerous Apps

While some apps may seem benign, you would be surprised to find that there are many that are dangerous to our tweens and teens. The technology is moving so fast that it may seem impossible to keep up. This is why it is so important that we keep ourselves educated. We have to remember that there is never any reason our kids need to be in hidden chat rooms or using anonymous texting. We also need to beware of the apps that help our kids hide things. If they have to hide it, you can bet they shouldn't be doing it.

When appropriate, we should make sure our kids have safety settings on their accounts to block bad content. It is within our right to periodically check to see what apps they have on their phones. We just don't want to get crazy about it.

At the end of the book, you will find our list of Apps of Concern as resources you can use to set limits, block inappropriate content, and keep them safe as well as resources to keep you up to date.

#5 Sexting

The term "sexting" is a combination of the words "sex" and "texting." Sexting is the transmission of nude, semi-nude, or sexually explicit material and sharing these images using mobile phones or by posting them on the internet and social media. [21]

Researchers surveyed 606 teens ages 14 to 18 and found that approximately 20 percent of the teens said they had sent a sexual image of themselves via cell phone. About twice as many teens admitted to receiving a sext. Of those who reported receiving a sext, well over 25 percent said that they had forwarded it to someone else.[22] So, they're sharing the pics with their friends.

Sadly, a third of the teens stated that they didn't think about the legal ramifications or consequences of their actions.

Here's what you can do to raise their awareness:

- Share real stories in the news to talk about sexting and the consequences.

- Discuss peer pressure and normalize the power it can have at this age.

- Share with them the legal consequences: in some states, underage sexting can be prosecuted as child pornography. In others, it's treated as a misdemeanor. Either way, it can land your teenager in legal trouble, but many teenagers don't know

---

21 If you'd like to understand more about sexting, here are links to two good articles that were live at the time of this writing: https://www.verywellfamily.com/what-is-sexting-problem-1258921
https://d5d67f66-6cc8-47c4-830f-e75ea3d9d064.filesusr.com/ugd/f6bccd_de59b266891d44ba8dd77a60a7e489d2.pdf

22 https://archive.unews.utah.edu/news_releases/u-study-finds-sending-sexually-explicit-photos-by-cell-phone-more-common-among-teen-than-you-might-think/

that. More than 60 percent of students in the Drexel study said they were unaware of the possible legal consequences.[23]

- More detailed information on the sexting laws in your state can be found here and in the resource section: https://cyber-bullying.org/state-sexting-laws.

- Remind them that once photos are out there you can't get them back.

- Go through "what if" scenarios:

  - Have you ever known someone who was asked to send a naked picture, or has anyone ever asked you to send a naked picture?

  - What would you do if you were asked to send a naked picture of yourself?

  - What if you send a sext and then regret it? Then what happens?

  - What if you break up with your boyfriend/girlfriend—what happens to those pictures?

  - How would you feel if you took a picture and it got passed around?

  - What would you do if someone sent you a picture of someone else that wasn't meant to be shared publicly?

- Remind them that once a picture is sent they have no control of where it winds up. Recipients can forward and share it without you even knowing about it and it can never be retrieved.

- Talk about pressures to send revealing photos. Let teens know that you understand how they can be pushed or dared into sending something. Explain to them that no matter how much pressure they feel to send a picture, the negative ramifications could be far worse.

---

23   https://yourteenmag.com/technology/teens-and-sexting

- Teach your children that if someone sends them a photo, they should delete it immediately. Encourage them to think about how they would feel if a picture was taken of them and passed around. Emphasize that it is never okay to ask or pressure anyone to sext, nor is it okay to send unsolicited sexts.

- Discuss peer pressure and provide strategies for how to say no. Ask them what they might say if someone pressured them and asked them to send a sext.

- Make sure they understand that they can come to you with questions or problems NO MATTER WHAT. No matter how inappropriate the content or how embarrassed they feel, they can come to you with no judgment or fear of getting in trouble.

What to do if you find sexting photos on your kid's phone:

- Be sensitive. As hard as it may be, stay calm and don't react in anger. This can cause them to shut down and not talk to you. Find ways to move beyond the anger before you talk to them.

- Stay calm and stay away from catastrophizing.

- Tell them what you found and then shut up and listen. Let them talk.

- Avoid shaming and don't threaten right then and there to take away their phone.

- Seek to understand what motivated them to send the sext. Remember what was mentioned in Chapter 5, about teens and tweens wanting to "fit in" and their desire for attention. Oftentimes they are feeling pressured and don't know how to say no. They also often don't think of the adverse consequences. They want attention and to feel special. The desire to be liked can be so strong at this age.

#6 Pornography

"Kids are curious about sex. Spoiler alert: this is normal and healthy. This natural curiosity can, unfortunately, be hijacked by easy-access pornography, which provides highly unrealistic and unhealthy depictions of 'sex,' and is a low-quality substitute for teaching what real relationships and real intimacy look like."[24]

When it comes to pornography, we can't be naive and think our kids will never see it. If they don't see it on their own device, there is a very good chance they will see it on one of their friends'. So, let's operate under the assumption that your kids will come across pornography, whether on purpose or by accident (it's not that hard to mistype into a search engine these days).

Then we need to talk to them about it sooner rather than later.

This is why it is so important to have that open dialogue. Your kids need to know you are a safe place when they see something they are concerned about. Don't freak out!

We want them to know they won't get into trouble because they saw it, and they won't be shamed or told they are bad or wrong. If we don't communicate about it—or we make our kids afraid of it—our children will be more likely to search it out.

It should also be said that if you haven't, you need to start talking to your kids about sex. (See the Resources Section for some helpful recommendations.) Your first conversation will set the tone for future conversations, so it's helpful to have a game plan for starting the conversation about pornography.

How to Talk to Your Kids about Pornography

Talking to our kids about pornography can make us all feel squeamish. Even though we may want to avoid the awkwardness, discomfort, and

---

24   https://fightthenewdrug.org/lets-talk-about-porn/blueprint/child-them/

fear of not knowing how to say the "right" thing about the dangers of pornography, we must push through those feelings. The reality is, the statistics are alarming when it comes to the chances your child will be exposed to pornography whether it's by accident or by being sexually curious. A nationally representative estimate of the percentage of U.S. youths (ages 14 to 18) exposed to pornography is 84.4 percent of males and 57 percent of females.[25]

Child and adolescent pornography exposure can be either intentional or unintentional. Examples of unintentional exposure include the opening of unsolicited messages or receiving spam emails, mis-typing website addresses, searching for terms that have a nonsexual as well as sexual meaning, or accidentally viewing pop-up images and advertisements.[26]

The greatest weapon we have in the battle to protect our kids from the harmful effects of pornography is to have on-going conversations that are open, non-shaming, honest, and loving.

The good news is that when we educate ourselves and learn how best to talk to our kids, we will feel more confident, equipped, and empowered to have these necessary conversations.

Here are a few things to keep in mind:

- Expect it will be awkward. This is totally normal!
- Give them a fair warning — something like, "We need to talk about internet pornography; there are a few things I want to be sure you know."
- A good way to start to break the ice is, "This is uncomfortable for me to talk about but it's important."
- Share what's true: "I know that a lot of kids are looking at porn online, but I'm hoping you won't. Sex can be mutual, loving, and

---

25   https://www.jpedhc.org/article/S0891-5245(19)30384-0/fulltext
26   Ibid

fulfilling, but it can also be dark and destructive. What you see in pornography is almost always the wrong kind of sex, and I don't want you to assume that pornography is what sex is all about."

- You might say: "There's another reason I don't want you looking at pornography. People often find that they get turned on by stuff and at the same time they feel bad watching it. I wouldn't want you to experience guilt and shame when something might 'feel' good but in your heart, you know it's wrong."

- Give them the facts: Pornography is exploitive. Those are real people in those images, whose vulnerabilities are being taken advantage of. People suffer tremendously from pornography.

- Talk about the difference between porn and healthy sex.

- Keep your relationship strong and invest in spending quality time and building a healthy relationship. Perhaps one of the greatest findings of all the research I found was "Adolescents who used pornography more frequently were male, at a more advanced pubertal stage, sensation seekers, and had weak or troubled family relations."[27]

What if your teen seems unconcerned about the dangers of porn? Many young people are under the misconception that porn is harmless. Here are some facts to point out:

- Porn is all about taking and abusing, manipulating, and exploiting others.

- Porn and sex trafficking are inseparably linked, and much of society denies or is unaware of this fact.[28]

---

27 https://www.tandfonline.com/doi/
    full/10.1080/00224499.2016.1143441?src=recsys
28 https://fightthenewdrug.org/sex-trafficking-and-porn-overlap/

- It sabotages the ability to enjoy normal sex and can lead to keeping secrets, shame, addiction, and serious relationship and marital issues.
- Sex in the context of a relationship of intimacy is about giving, serving, loving, and sacrificing.
- We were designed for intimacy and connection. We were made to love and be loved, to know and be known.
- Porn can leave you feeling very lonely, whereas being known and truly loved, respected and valued by another person, is so fulfilling.

While limiting access to porn can be challenging, there are steps that you can take to be proactive to keep them safe. Talk to them and use filters to block pornographic content. Don't be naive to think your kid won't be exposed. Even though it's awkward and uncomfortable, start by admitting it's uncomfortable to talk about pornography but you feel it's important. Admit what's true—that a lot of kids at this age are curious and are looking at pornography and it's important to talk about pornography, even though it's uncomfortable. Explain how pornography exploits others and can also be dark and destructive and that it's not what sex is all about—plus, it can become an addiction. Make sure to listen to what they have to say and let them know that porn can cause people to experience guilt and shame and keep secrets because they know deep down it's wrong. Express that you don't want this for them and your hope is that they will feel free to talk about it with either you, their other parent, or someone they trust.

CHAPTER SEVEN

GAMING

"I manage a 911 center. The entire industry nationwide is understaffed. These are good paying jobs with great benefits. I will hire gamers—All. Day. Long. Their tech skills are top notch and their multitasking is superb, all skills I need for them to have to save lives."
~Mandy B., Moms of Tweens and Teens Community

"There is no doubt lots of fun energy and bonding can happen over video games. They can even inspire people to make changes to improve their lives."
~Delaney Ruston, MD, Creator of
the Award-Winning Film *Screenagers*

O nline gaming can be a love/hate relationship for most parents. I love what Jen Kehl, CEO of Moms of Tweens and Teens, shared on our blog, which about sums up the realities of gaming and how most moms feel:

> *"I constantly have to remind myself that laughing mania-cally, intermittent yelps, and trash talking are normal things coming from my son's bedroom. I get frustrated when my son is called for dinner, and the answer inevitably is, 'Mom, I'm in a game. I'll be out when I die.'"*

Jen goes on to say,

> *"In the grand scheme of things, I try to remind myself that he is home, his homework is done, and he's happy and engaged. He's the full package of a great son. So he comes late and eats cold food for dinner. Is it really that bad?"*

If you have a gamer in your home, you may be relating to the frustration and guilt you can feel. Moms often share with me that they understand that gaming today is a huge part of how their kids connect with their friends. At the same time, they struggle with knowing how much is too much and worry about the long-term impact.

You may be asking yourself,

"Is it okay that they're playing for hours on end?"

"How much is too much?"

"How do I get my kid to play less and get them out of the house?"

"Is Fortnite okay for my kid to play?"

These are all valid and important questions to answer. But before we answer them, there are a few things you need to understand first.

The Positives of Gaming

1. **Gaming can be a valid concern for parents and a source of tension with families, but it's also not all bad.**

"We often thought gaming was the devil in our house.
Long hours of yelling, staring at the screen, grades
that were so-so. BUT, what we didn't know was that my son's
skill set and learned multitasking on multiple screens
would set him up for his dream job. Gaming isn't all bad."
~Lisa, Mom of a Son Now in His Twenties

Studies have found that videos can improve learning. Many video games teach kids how to work as a team, collaborate, and strategize to beat the level. They are a way they connect with their friends and meet new people. "The Federation of American Scientists (FAS) argues that kids need to play *more* video games in order to be competitive in the current job market. In a report they released in 2010, the FAS said games helped teach higher-order thinking skills like problem solving, interpretive analysis, and more."[29]

2. **Gaming in large part is how kids connect today with their friends.**

According to Pew Research, "Playing games can have the effect of reinforcing a sense of friendship and connectedness for teens who play online with friends. Nearly eight in 10 online-gaming teens (78 percent) say they feel more connected to existing friends they play games with. For teen boys, this is especially true–84 percent of boys who play networked games say they feel more connected to friends when they play, compared with 62 percent of girls."[30]

---

29   https://www.uvpediatrics.com/topics/video-games-pros-and-cons/
30   https://www.pewresearch.org/internet/2015/08/06/chapter-3-video-games-are-key-elements-in-friendships-for-many-boys/

While you may find it weird and hard to understand how your kid can spend hours playing a video game on a monitor with headphones yelling at their friends, it's their world today. It's where their friends are. It's our version of bingeing on Netflix or getting lost in a good book. To us it might be ludicrous, but to them it is virtually the same. Gaming is one of the ways kids interact and communicate with friends. Their social landscape is different today than when we were growing up.

3. **Gaming is how they decompress.**

According to Pew Research, "A larger percentage of teens say playing games allows them to feel more relaxed and happy than the percentage who report anger and frustration. Fully 82 percent of teens say they feel relaxed and happy when they play, with 86 percent of boys and 72 percent of girls reporting these experiences." [31]

We may not get it, because, seriously, how can screaming and yelling calm someone down? Screaming into headphones and shooting things on a screen would significantly raise our stress levels. But what works for our kids often doesn't work for us.

After a long day at school or in the middle of studying, it is a valid way that kids can relax and decompress. It can ease the struggle of adolescent stress and benefit them to focus on something else, and relax.

4. **They want to be good.**

Who wants to be the worst on the team? No one. And this is how our kids feel regarding gaming—they don't want to stink.

---

31   https://www.pewresearch.org/internet/2015/08/06/chapter-3-video-games-are-key-elements-in-friendships-for-many-boys/

Many kids feel like gaming is something they excel at. It builds their confidence and gives them a feeling of mastery. You may cringe listening to them yelling and barking directions and orders but in their mind they are being leaders and they want to do well. It always feels good to know you can do something well, even if that something isn't what we perceive to be as valuable as excelling at a sport or in an activity. However, it is important to them.

With the high levels of stress and the pressures to succeed in our adolescents' world today, having something they are truly good at has to feel like a boost. It is always soul building to do something truly well.

The Negatives about Gaming

While video games can play a positive role in our kids' lives, they can also cause problems.

How do you know when the amount of gaming time is too much?

- It's impacting their school work.
- They aren't getting chores or homework done.
- Grades are dropping.
- They aren't getting enough sleep.
- Most of their time is spent gaming—they aren't getting together with friends outside of gaming, they aren't participating in other activities.
- They aren't engaging with family.
- They aren't moving their bodies or getting physical exercise.
- They are experiencing increased anxiety, irritability, and anger.

These are also signs that your tween or teen needs limits on the amount of time they are spending gaming. The key again here is to find balance. If the amount of time they are gaming is getting in the way of homework, getting good sleep, participating in other activities, getting some physical exercise, or spending time with friends and family, and if you notice irritability, anger, or anxiety, be proactive and set limits.

> *"Certain things have to be done before gaming or free time anyways, like homework and chores, etc. Plus, if we— the parents—want it to be family time, that comes first too. But if we are just hanging out, not doing much, then they can play all day if they want to. We are also an outdoors family so they do get their fill of hunting, fishing, camping, etc., plus school activities."*
> ~Alyssa, Mom of Teens

Setting up Parameters

If you're concerned that gaming is getting in the way of their responsibilities, other activities, or spending face to face time with others, here are some steps you can take:

1. **Sit down and have a conversation.**

Here's a helpful formula to start the discussion:

Share what you're noticing (the problem).
"I'm noticing that you're gaming on school nights and not getting your homework done."

Express what you want.
"I want to make sure you are getting your homework done before you get gaming time."

Ask them for their thoughts.

"How are you thinking this might work?"

"What do you think is a reasonable amount of gaming time in order to get your work done?"

Listen to their thoughts without judgment.

2. **Negotiate to set up a reasonable amount of time to play video games.**

When setting a reasonable time limit, rather than completely withholding screen time we came up with the "if you, then you" formula, which seems to work well. "If you____, then you _____." For example, *"If you* get your homework and chores done, *then you* can have two hours of gaming time.

Some kids like to game with their friends to decompress right after school. If this is the case, you might say something like, "**If you** can prove to me that you can game right after school and get your work done afterwards, **then you** can continue to play after school. However, **if you're** not getting your work done, **then we** will have to come up with another plan."

Here are some other questions to consider when setting gaming limits (and to discuss with your tween or teen):

- How much gaming will you allow on school nights, weekends, summer nights, and school breaks?
- Do they need to contribute around the house or get their homework done before they can have gaming time?
- What time do they need to be off at night in order to get a good night's sleep?

How to Connect around Gaming

#1 Explore the Good Parts of Gaming

Engage your kids in conversation about the healthy aspects about the games they play. As a prompt, ask about specific elements often found in gaming, such as learning new information, teamwork, and strategy. If you're game savvy yourself, it might also be helpful to talk about specific aspects of games that you think are positive.

#2 Consider the Not-So-Good Parts of Gaming

Now ask them if there are ever times where gaming makes them feel bad or causes conflict with family or friends. Have they ever encountered bullying or threatening language while playing a game?

This is also a good time to talk about feeling "left out" if they don't play a certain game or if they have to log off before finishing a level.

#3 Brainstorm Positive Ways to Game

Talk about ways gaming can benefit your kids when done in a balanced way. Maybe gaming can help them improve at a sport because they better understand the strategies. Maybe it can help with hand-eye coordination or reflexes. Or maybe it can inspire an offline activity with their friends.

#4 Play Games Together

Gaming comes in many different forms — some may be more positive than others. To better understand the nuances of your kid's games, try playing as a family.

#5 Understand Online Gaming

Many games can now be played against other people (including strangers). Consider this in relation to your kid's level of maturity and ability to judge who they should be engaging with.

Here are some questions to discuss with them:

- What is your favorite game to play and what do you like about it?
- How much time do you think you should be allowed on school nights or over the weekend?
- What needs to be done before you can spend time gaming?

CHAPTER EIGHT

FACE TIME VERSUS SCREEN TIME

"Miss your teens? Turn off the wifi and they will come
pouring out of their rooms faster than you can say,
'I don't know what happened.'"
~Moms of Tweens and Teens

"Your cell phone has already replaced your camera,
your calendar, your alarm clock…
Don't let it replace your family."
~ @snapconf

By now we understand that technology is here to stay. We may not like the hours of time our kids want to be on their phones or playing video games. We know they need limits. But we can't stop there. It's important we get intentional and find different ways to connect with our kids.

Here are some ideas to make face time a meaningful and enjoyable experience for everyone, including your oftentimes resistant tweens and teens.

#1 Provide Family Fun Alternatives

Helping your children manage the amount of time they are on their devices is much easier when they have alternatives. Sometimes the best way to provide alternatives is to find activities that are fun and entertaining for the whole family.

Think outside of the box. What are some activities that are fun and different that we can do with our kids? I have a friend who recently took her girls on the L-train to a museum in downtown Chicago — just for the pure adventure of it.

Get your kids to come up with a bucket list of fun activities they'd like to try or do and stick it on the refrigerator and check it off.

Get everybody on board by allowing your kids a turn to suggest the next activity.

I have learned to be persistent. Often my kids will initially balk at my ideas yet change their tone after the fact. Recently I had an adventure with my daughters who fought me tooth and nail, only to have them thank me later for the fun day.

#2 Take Ten

Taking time to connect with your teen doesn't have to be stressful or a big deal. I know my kids feel uncomfortable when I come at them with this type of energy. I find ten minutes a day is a good touch point to start with. We can ask our kids to put away their cell phones during the ride to school or practice. When our kids are adolescents, think quality, not quantity.

#3 Seize the Moment When an Opportunity Presents Itself

When, seemingly out of the blue, one of my kids starts to talk to me, I have to remind myself to stop, look, and listen. I literally say to myself, *Quit washing dishes, put the phone down, and turn away from your laptop. Stop!* It's not easy for me to transition when I am "in the zone." It takes a conscious reminder that this is a precious moment and I need to seize the opportunity.

#4 Be Present and Enjoy Your Kids

> *"Teenagers talk about the idea of having each other's full attention. They grew up in a culture of distraction. They remember their parents were on cell phones when they were pushed on swings as toddlers. Now, their parents text at the dinner table and don't look up from their BlackBerry when they come for end-of-school day pickup."*
> ~Sherry Turkle

This quote above makes me feel sad, a little scared, and angry. But it also begs the question: what are we modeling for our kids? Are we actually awake when we're with them, putting down our phones when they come to talk to us, looking them in the eye, and genuinely interested in what they have to say? If I answered honestly, my answer would sometimes be no; it's easy for me to get distracted too.

Our kids need our attention perhaps like never before. In a world where there's so many distractions, where they want to fit in and belong, where they're looking outside of themselves to define who they are, they need us to be there for them. And not only do they need us to be there for them, they need us to enjoy being with them.

I'll never forget the time I asked my tween daughter what meant the most to her. I was surprised by her answer, "When you laugh at my jokes." Of all the things she could have named, she named how I made her feel. When I laughed at her jokes she knew without a doubt I was enjoying her company. I understand if you're reading this and you're struggling to enjoy your kid. These years can be challenging no doubt about it AND I want to challenge you: look for different ways to enjoy your tween or teen.

It begins with us becoming the kind of parent that our kids want to talk to and spend time with. I find the 80/20 formula to be a great place to start when it comes to building connection and enjoying our kids. Here's the formula: Listen 80 percent. Talk 20 percent. It's amazing the difference it makes when we are quiet and choose to shut up and listen. We need to stop giving advice and lecturing and listen instead.

As parents, it's easy to assume we know our kids and yet there is so much going on in their world we don't know about. When you listen, you can learn so much more about them, their inner and outer world, and their perspective. They have so much to say and are more insightful and wiser than we often give them credit for. And, you might discover as I have that they have a lot to teach you if you're only open to listening. Enjoying your kids requires that you withhold judgment, criticism, or giving unsolicited advice and look for ways to connect on their terms.

When and where do they tend to open up and talk? It's often when you're on car rides, walking the dog together, sitting down with them when they play a video game (or playing it with them), asking them to show you their favorite YouTube video, playing music in the car together, going out for breakfast, or doing whatever they enjoy. And if you don't know, ask them.

#5 Provide Downtime

Kids need to have unstructured time, and technology adds an additional layer to our kids not getting downtime to just *be*. These days, kids don't have the opportunity to be bored, relax, and just play.

While developing interests, talents, and hobbies is a good thing, and these things play an important role in kids' lives, many kids today are overscheduled with organized teams and clubs. Make sure you give your kids unstructured time to be alone, even if they complain about being bored. They need the space to watch the clouds go by, to be present with themselves, and learn how to be comfortable in their own skin.

Take Time to Talk in "Real Time"

Following are some discussion questions intended to build a stronger relationship with your kids. When you are intentional about making time for real conversations, your kids will know that you care and want to hear their thoughts, feelings, and what they have to say. You are laying a foundation to increase the likelihood that they will feel safe to come and talk to you if they are having an issue or are exposed to inappropriate content.

These questions will also help your tween or teen become more self-aware and will strengthen their self-monitoring skills. When you have these discussions, it's important to withhold judgment and remember the bigger vision of creating a strong relationship for years to come.

Here are some questions to help you, the parent, get clarity first:

- What are your biggest areas of concern/angst?
- What values do you want to cultivate and uphold in your family?
- What are the main reasons (your why) behind the limits and ground rules you want to set?
- Where might you need to educate yourself?
- What answers do you need to move forward and be proactive?
- Why do you care how much time your kids spend on their screens?

Guidelines for Phone/Device Use in Daily Life

Tweens and teens who are included in the decision-making process are more likely to comply with the limits. This doesn't mean you have to make your limits solely based on their input. The goal here is to let them know what they think matters to you. Here are some questions and thoughts to discuss with your children that can help you establish guidelines for phone and device use:

- What are your family values regarding time together and relating to one another?
- How do you think screen time should fit into your lives—as individuals and as a family?
- How much time do you think is appropriate when it comes to balancing homework and outside activities?
- Do you think online entertainment, gaming, and/or social media are getting in the way of doing other things, like spending time with friends, exploring other interests, being physically active, schoolwork, or participating in extracurricular activities?
- How many hours per day should your children be allowed "screen time" for entertainment (not including schoolwork)?
- Are your children allowed to have their phones with them when they go to bed at night? (not recommended) Where will the phones be kept/charged overnight?
- Are phones allowed at the dinner table?
- Can they be on their phones while riding as a passenger in a car with other family members?
- Are there other parameters regarding where/when they may or may not use their phones or devices?

Discussing as a family:

- What times and places do we agree it's important to be focused and present with one another?
- When is it important that you/we be focused? During homework? When we're together as a family? During chores? At dinner?
- What changes do we need to make that would create more balance in our family and as individuals?
- Is there a time in the day when we'd like to unplug and be together?

Talking to Your Kids about Social Media and Gaming

- How does social media make you feel?
- What do you like? What don't you like?
- What do you like about Instagram or your video game?
- How do you feel when you're looking at other people's Instagram feeds?
- How do you feel when you're gaming or done gaming?
- Do you remember a time when you were distracted and missed something because you were on your phone?
- Have you experienced others (friends or family) not being fully present with you? How did that feel?
- Have you missed something significant because you were distracted by technology? How did you feel afterwards?

Get to know what they like and create connection with your kids. Here are some conversation starters:

- What apps do you like best?
- What's your favorite YouTube channel?

- What's your favorite video game?
- Can you show me? Tell me more about what you like about it.

Discuss the dangers and downsides of online social interactions with them. Let them know:

- People aren't always who they say they are. Even someone you meet on social media and chat with for months might be lying about their identity. Don't post your location publicly.
- If someone, even a friend, makes you feel uncomfortable, tell me about it. We'll discuss what we need to do about it, and I won't make any decisions about it without your input.
- Don't share any nude or suggestive photos with anyone, even if you know and trust the person. Sometimes these photos get stolen or intentionally shared or posted publicly.
- Devices can sometimes cause people to miss out on things that matter to them. Touch on the times when you weren't fully "there" because you were on your phone.
- Talk about what your own goals are regarding social media and if they think they could benefit from setting a goal for themselves.

Talk about how they think social media impacts their friendships:

- Do you think social media has made our society more social or less social?
- What are some of your favorite things to do with friends online? Face to face?
- Do you have friends you consider close but with whom you mostly interact online?
- Whom would you like to spend more time with in person?

One of our greatest desires and callings in life is to raise our kids to be good humans. And, we want to have great relationships with our kids. We don't want to be nagging and lecturing and fighting about the amount of time they are on their devices (although to be realistic, there will be some of that).We want to savor these years. But in our world where screen time is replacing face-to-face time and online connections are competing for real connections, it's challenging.

To say that it's easy to feel overwhelmed navigating our kids' technology today is an understatement. We can feel resentful about the time they spend on their digital devices. We can worry and hover out of fear about the risks and negative content they might be exposed to and how to best keep them safe.

We want to raise them to be responsible digital citizens and we care deeply about their emotional well-being. We want them to thrive emotionally and socially. We want them to become their best selves and to grow up to have meaningful relationships and live their best lives. And it can feel like technology is getting in the way of all of these things.

Even though it's true that navigating our tween and teen's technological world can be daunting, what matters most is for you to remember that you are the most important and influential person in your kid's life (even though they might not show it). When it comes to managing, monitoring, and setting limits, put your relationship with them first. Rather than resenting the amount of time they spend online, remember this is the world that they live in. Instead of nagging and trying to control things (which is so easy to do), talk with them about expectations and setting healthy limits. Use some of the questions I've presented in this book to ask them meaningful questions as a way to connect with them. Ask them what they think and how they feel about their digital world. Sprinkle these conversations into daily conversations when the time is right and listen to what they have to say without judgment.

When we focus on being proactive and investing in building a strong relationship with our kids—listening more than talking, putting aside our judgment, being curious to hear what they think and entering into their digital world—they will begin to open up and be more receptive to our expectations and limits. Rather than focusing on the negative stuff, focus on the positive things your kid does on a daily basis (no matter how small) and affirm them for it. Believe me, they need it. Cultivate more of the good stuff—spending time having fun, finding simple ways to connect, inviting them to share their favorite YouTube channel, or sending them a funny text. Use technology in positive ways and allow it to become a friend, not a foe. Model this in your own life and put down your phone or take a break from your computer to look them in the eye.

Make these changes in how you approach technology in your life, and it will make all the difference in the choices they make in theirs

SHOULD I READ MY KIDS' TEXTS?

Not long ago, I sat down to research and compile a list of the best apps for protecting kids on their cell phones, and came upon an article entitled, "The 5 Best Apps for Spying on Your Teen."

This title didn't sit well with me.

Now, who of us hasn't read our kid's texts? I know I have, and I've found out a lot of valuable information that I wouldn't have discovered if I hadn't.

Reading my kid's texts has left me feeling proud, horrified, validated, and more anxious than before I started, all at the same time:

- I've felt proud when they've shown such maturity and wisdom in their responses when their friends have texted them with their problems.
- I was surprised and laughed out loud at their wit and humor.
- I've had the wool yanked from my eyes and seen through my rose-colored glasses to what was really going on.

- My gut instincts have been validated.
- "Yep, that kid's trouble."
- "Yep, they weren't telling the truth."
- "Yep, I need to say no to that sleepover."
- "Yep, there's drinking going on."

We may have a laundry list of valid reasons for reading our kid's texts:

- "It's my right as the parent; I'm paying for the darn thing."
- "There's cyber-bullying and it's a scary world out there; it's my job to protect my child and to keep them safe."
- "If they're drinking, doing drugs, or looking at pornography, I need to know about it."
- "At the very least I want to know if they've arrived safely at their destination."
- "God forbid how guilty I'd feel if I didn't know they were being cyber-bullied, sexting, doing drugs, or if a creepy person was talking to them!"

Monitoring our kids' cell phones is just part of being a good parent in a digital age, right?

Not so fast.

Now, lest you start pointing your finger at me lecturing me about all the dangers, let me just say, I'm fully aware the struggle is real! But while I'm an advocate of being proactive to protect our kids, I want us to examine our reasons a little further before we download our monitoring apps and read our kid's texts.

Every time I hear about a mom that is reading her kids texts nightly, I have a strong reaction.

I've been that mom and I regret it. Yes, you're hearing me right: if you're reading their texts every night, I'm challenging you to stop it.

With my oldest, texting hadn't been invented. MySpace was the thing at the time. I was scared (freaking out better describes it). My teen was hanging with the "wrong" crowd, and I didn't know what to do. I wanted to know what was going on so I could protect my kid from bad things happening. So, I downloaded an app (it was called a *program* at the time, with an accompanying DVD) and I was sent daily emails that shared every comment and conversation. My choice to download that program was not a good thing. In fact, it caused greater distress and problems.

One of the reasons I'm so passionate about this topic is that I've experienced the damage it does to our relationships when we parent from a place of fear and anxiety. *When fear is in the driver's seat, ultimately, it's not going to steer you in the right direction.*

Reading my daughter's texts didn't protect her or keep bad things from happening. In fact, it hurt my relationship with my daughter. The more I read my daughter's texts, the more over-the-top my reactions became, the less my teen wanted to talk to me, and the more suspicious I became. My fear got worse and the distance between us became greater.

Now that you've heard my story, here are five questions to ask yourself as you wonder if you should read your tween or teen's texts.

1. Are you putting your relationship first?

I never thought about this back in my teen's MySpace day. When an adolescent gets the message that you're infringing on their privacy and becoming overly involved in their life, it will cause a rift in your relationship. That's why one of the most important things we can ask ourselves as parents is, "What am I doing that is conducive to creating a closer relationship?"

I'm not saying we are to be our kids' friends. What I'm challenging you to ask yourself is, "What are the consequences of potentially damaging the trust in my relationship with my child?"

More than anything else, parenting is about *relationship*. After coaching moms for over a decade, I've learned that many of the parenting issues we struggle with stem from a disconnect in the relationship. When we focus on our relationship first, we increase the chances that our kids will listen to what we have to say.

2. **Are you checking your kid's texts because you're driven by fear, or do you have valid reasons?**

I remember, as a teen, stretching the hallway phone cord as far as I could to get the phone into my room and shutting the door. If my mom would have listened to my conversations as a teen, I'm sure she would have probably gone nuts and not let me leave the house.

There's just some stuff that is better for us to not know about.

Much of our teens' conversations is innocent talk fueled by the fact that they're trying to figure out who they are. Our teens need space. We're a generation of parents who are way too overly involved and into our kid's business because *we are parenting by fear*.

I can understand checking texts more often when we're concerned about our kids doing drugs, or because something is clearly amiss and they're not talking, or because we are heeding the signs that they're in potential danger. But we need to know the difference between parenting by fear and being a responsible parent.

3. **Are you looking for information because your kid isn't communicative?**

Being less communicative is part of being a teen. For moms, this is unsettling. I've found myself peeking at texts not out of a place of concern; rather, I want to know what's going on because they tell me so little.

I've had moms share how they read their teens' texts because they're concerned about their social lives and if they have any friends, which only leads them to ask their teens unhelpful questions. They've decided to stop it and so have I. It's difficult, but we need to resist doing this.

So, what does it mean to be a responsible parent when it comes to our kids' cell phones? How much monitoring is too much? Where do we draw the line? We need to be aware of when we're reacting rather than being proactive. We need to talk about the tough topics and our expectations and rules surrounding their smartphones.

I like what Josh Shipp says: "What we need to do is empower our kids to make good decisions with this new gadget—to help them understand that a cell phone, like all privileges, is a responsibility." We should stay informed about the apps we don't want on our kid's phones.

We should make sure our kids have safety settings on their accounts so bad content is blocked.

And, it *is* within our right to periodically check to see what apps they have on their phones; we just don't want to get crazy about it.

If you have fallen into the practice of regularly reading your children's texts, I implore you to not continue. Let's not allow fear to get in the way of building stronger relationships with our teens. Let's instead be proactive to stay informed, set up house rules, and be discerning on what it means to keep them safe in our digital world. More importantly, let's talk to our kids and build stronger relationships with them first. Let's have the important discussions and find opportunities to connect so we know how they're doing.

What's the message we're sending our kids when we read their texts? The most damaging message I was sending my oldest child was, "I don't trust you," and, "You're bad," when I was constantly reacting out of my fear. I can't stress enough the power we have in our kids' lives over who they grow up to believe they are. When we believe in our kids' ability to make good decisions, chances are they will.

I still catch myself when I'm saying something that is not sending my youngest, also a teen, the message that I believe in her and trust her to make good decisions. I try to tell her often, "I believe you have the wisdom inside of you to make good decisions. I trust you to do that."

Try it. There is a change in their whole demeanor. You can see them taking it in and standing a little taller—and, hopefully, rising to the level of the trust you are placing in them.

PROTECTING YOUR KIDS ONLINE

https://www.commonsensemedia.org/blog/
parents-ultimate-guide-to-parental-controls

I don't believe in spying—or sneaking your child's phone out of their bedroom—but I also don't think handing over what's basically a super-charged portal to the internet is smart either. Coupling this with my lack of tech savvy, I've struggled with giving sound product recommendations. Sanity isn't about "watching" what they are doing on their phones, instead it's about safety and managing how they use them.

Different tech solutions and programs are appropriate for different situations. Don't be afraid to dig in. All of these programs that I recommend have very robust customer service (that's a huge reason why I recommend them!). Their goal is to make sure that you succeed. Also, don't be afraid to mix and match solutions. Not every solution will be the perfect fit. Sometimes you need a combination—e.g., you can use Screentime and Disney Circle and Xbox built-in controls.

"Using a monitoring service is helpful to setting limits and protecting your kids, but there is one thing that is more effective than any program you will have and it's free. It's you."
Delaney Ruston, Documentary Filmmaker of *Screenagers* and Primary Care Physician

Remember: digital tools and settings can help you stay on top of your kid's online life, but they can't replace staying involved, having conversations, and helping them make responsible choices.

What Are the Best Parental Controls for iPhone, iPad, or Android?

Finding the right apps to meet your specific needs can be a confusing and overwhelming endeavor. So, we (Jen Kehl, our Social Media Director here at Moms of Tweens and Teens and I) have done the research to help you find the most effective ways to control and monitor your child's screen time and to keep them safe. Understand that these programs are always updating, improving, and changing. And, there are a lot of differing opinions on which one is the best. The list we have put together is based on some of the most (currently) highly rated parental controls and systems as well as feedback from parents in our community.

Due to the overwhelming plethora of parental control options, before you dive in, I recommend that you figure out what your specific needs are (i.e., Do you want to block unwanted content such as pornography? Track your kids' location to make sure they make it safely home from school? Set up limits during homework time? Block apps that you don't want them accessing due to their age?) Getting very clear about what and why you want to use parental controls will help you when deciding the best programs for your kid(s) and family.

One of the best websites I know to stay updated on recommended Parental Controls is Common Sense Media—https://www.common sensemedia.org/blog/parents-ultimate-guide-to-parental-controls.

Parental Control Apps That Offer Free Parental Control Tools

I love this tested and reviewed overview on the best parental control software for 2021 from TechJury based on specific needs:[32]

- Qustodio - Best cross-platform option
- Bark - Best for social media monitoring
- McAfee Safe Family - Best for Windows
- Mobicip - Best for ChromeBook
- mSpy - Best for mobile phones
- Net Nanny - Best for location tracking
- Norton Family - Best parental control app for IOS
- OpenDNS FamilyShield - Best for blocking adult content
- KidLogger - Best for Android
- Spyrix Free Keylogger - Best for parental monitoring
- Kaspersky Safe Kids - Best mobile features and for PC

Block Websites and Filter Content

If you want to prevent access to specific websites and limit your kid's exposure to inappropriate content such as mature games or porn, you can use the parental controls that are built into your device's operating system. Every major operating system—Microsoft's Windows, Apple's Mac OS, and even Amazon's Fire—offers settings to keep kids from accessing stuff you don't want them to see. To get the benefits, you

---

32   https://www.techradar.com/best/parental-control

need to use the most updated version of the operating system, and each user has to log in under his or her profile.[33]

Best Parental Controls to Block Porn - A great article from Common Sense Media to help you protect your kids from pornography—https://www.commonsensemedia.org/blog/5-ways-to-block-porn-on-your-kids-devices

Best Parental Controls to Monitor Your Kid's Phone - To keep tabs on your tween or teen's phone, your best bet is to download an app to monitor text messages, social networks, emails, and other mobile functions—try Bark, Circle, TeenSafe, or WebWatcher. These are especially helpful if you're concerned about potentially risky conversations or iffy topics your kid might be engaging in. Bark, for example, notifies you when it detects "alert" words, such as "drugs." To monitor social media, you'll need your kid's account information, including passwords.[34]

Best Parental Controls to Track Your Kid's Location -

Life360 - One of the most popular tracking apps. This is available on Android and iOS, with a free tier that can show you not only the location of your child, but everyone in your family. Life360 allows you to organize people into Circles, which are essentially groups. The map displays where all the people are at all times.

---

33 https://www.commonsensemedia.org/blog/parents-ultimate-guide-to-parental-controls#What%20are%20the%C2%A0best%20network%20parental%20controls?

34 https://www.commonsensemedia.org/blog/parents-ultimate-guide-to-parental-controls

Google Maps - A free and easy way to keep up with where your kids are going, Google Maps has a built-in feature that allows people to share their location with others for an hour or indefinitely. It all works within the Google Maps app, so there's no need to add any additional software or pay any fees.

Apple Find My - Used to be called Find My Friends and is now called Find My as it also encompasses Find My iPhone. What's really cool is it can also it can also help you find your iPhone, iPad, Apple Watch, or AirPods by getting them to make a loud noise.

Find My Kids - You can set locations so you receive notifications when your child comes home, goes to school, or visits any set location. You'll know where they are and won't have to check it as often. You can view the exact history of locations for the day so that you know where they walk and what route they take to school. Your child can send an SOS signal if they are in danger and cannot call you. You can also listen to what is happening around your child.

Best Parental Controls to Control Your Home Network and Your home Wi-Fi - Wifi routers are another way to monitor content and manage screen time. Instead of installing software on all of your kids' PCs and tablets, parental control routers let you set up content filters right at the borders of your home network, so they can be easily applied to every device in your house.

Here are some articles to check out:

https://www.lifewire.com/best-802-11ac-wi-fi-wireless-routers-818077

https://www.clevguard.com/parental-control/parental-control-routers/

Best Parental Controls To Block Websites, Filter Content, Set Time Limits, And Monitor What Kids Are Doing Online

Bark - Bark helps families manage and protect their children's online lives. We monitor 30+ of the most popular apps and social media platforms, including text messaging and email, for signs of digital dangers. Our screen time management and web filtering tools help you set healthy limits around how and when your kids use their devices.

- Monitor content - Get alerts for issues like bullying, predators, sexual content, and more
- Manage screen time - Create custom daily screen time schedules for your child's device
- Filter websites - Block access to specific websites or even whole categories

Bark provides:

- Social Media Monitoring - Bark tracks conversations and content on Snapchat, Instagram, YouTube, Facebook, Twitter, Pinterest, GroupMe, and more
- Text and Email Monitoring - Bark works with iOS and Android to monitor texts, photos, and videos for concerning interactions
- Screen Time and Web Filtering - Manage when your kids can access the internet and which sites are appropriate for them to visit
- 24/7 Detection - Looks for activity that may indicate online predators, adult content, sexting, cyberbullying, drug use, suicidal thoughts, and more

- Parental Alerts - Get automatic alerts when Bark detects potential issues, along with expert recommendations from child psychologists for addressing them
- Time Saving and Trust Building - Saves you from manually monitoring your child's activities, respecting your time and your child's privacy by only surfacing potential concerns

(Visit this site for an extensive overview of what Bark monitors—https://www.bark.us/what-bark-monitors)

Meet Circle - Internet and Website Filtering. Customize settings to limit what can be viewed online for individual family members by choosing age-appropriate (or blocking inappropriate) app and website content for social media, video and gaming apps, and more.

Circle allows you to:

- Choose a filter level for each member of the family that's totally customizable for their age and interests. You can also customize what's right to keep your family safe online, and set healthy time limits and filter content—across every device—from one simple app. Circle's award-winning parental controls let you manage screen time and monitor not just some but ALL websites and apps. They have a complete in-home and on-the-go solution, you set the rules for sites like You-Tube, TikTok, Discord, and many more across all your family's connected devices.
- Connect with your router with their Circle Home Plus device to manage every internet-connected device on your home network.
- Use the Circle App to operate Circle and manage mobile devices (iOS and Android) everywhere.

- Limit screen time and block content on iPhones, Chromebooks, Android devices, and more, and includes the device plus an app subscription with access to all features.
- Have a bird's-eye view of all things internet, allowing you to review your family's online time, site visits, app usage, and even the current location of your kids.

Circle Go provides settings such as:

- **Time Limits** - Set specific time limits for specific apps and categories.
- **Off Time** - You can have multiple off times for homework, car rides, etc. You can even have different off times on different days.
- **Bedtime** - This includes specific bedtime limits; you can set different bedtimes on different days.
- **Filter** - This filters out content based on what level you want your child to see. This is a great place to put content restrictions on YouTube; it will also filter out any pornography, suicide-related content, etc. It is very robust. You can also block specific apps here.
- **Pause** - If at any time you decide your child needs a break, whether it's behavior or a specific event for which you haven't set up a downtime, you just hit the pause button, and it goes off.
- And more…

(Visit this site for an extensive overview of what Meet Circle monitors: https://meetcircle.com/)

Kaspersky Safe Kids - Provides parental control software for Windows, macOS, Android, iOS devices, with both free and paid-for versions.

- Manage your kids' screen time per day, per device to fit their schedule and your style of parenting
- Locate your kids wherever they go
- Block adult content and customize a list of sites and apps your child can only visit with your permission
- View your kids' YouTube search history & stop them searching for inappropriate adult topics

Kaspersky provides:

- **GPS Tracking** - Locate your kids wherever they go. Plus set a safe area for them to stay in and get alerted if they leave it. Track and pinpoint your kids' whereabouts 24/7 on a digital map inside your app. Set an area you want your kids to stay in, and get notified if they step outside it.
- **Screen-time controls** - Set a permitted number of hours of screen time per day and block the device if the limit is reached. Stop devices being used during specific time slots, like when your child should be doing homework
- **Website and App Filters** - Block access to age-inappropriate apps and websites using categories like Gambling, Violence, or Weapons. Limit app use by time and create a list of apps your kids need your permission to open.
- **YouTube Safe Search** - Monitor your kids' YouTube searches to ensure their online habits are healthy. Block search requests against harmful adult topics like alcohol, tobacco, and gambling.

(Visit this site for an extensive overview of what Kaspersky monitors: https://usa.kaspersky.com/)

Net Nanny -

- Instant Reporting of Online Searches
- Visibility to Apps Used by Your Kids
- Real-time Alerts on Porn, Suicide, Weapons, and Drug-related Content

Net Nanny features:

- **Screen Time Management** - Tailor your family's screen time and set specific hours of the day when your child can be online
- **Block Pornography** - Limit exposure to adult content or block pornography in real time
- **Website Blocker** - Block websites based on settings you can tailor to each of your family member's individual needs
- **Alerts and Reporting** - Review detailed reports and set up alerts about your child's online activity
- **Block Apps** - See which apps your child is using and block apps you don't want them to have access to
- **Family Feed** - Get insight and visibility into your family's online activity, in real-time, with the Net Nanny® Family Feed
- **Track Location** - Get peace of mind knowing that you are informed of your child's primary mobile device location in real time
- **Social Media Protection** - Protect your children on various social apps like Tik Tok, Instagram, Tumblr, Facebook, and more
- **Parent Dashboard** - Access the Net Nanny® Parent Dashboard from any device with a web browser and Internet Access to manage your family's account

- **YouTube Monitoring** - See YouTube video names, video length, view date, and even review the video with a direct link to each viewed video

(Visit this site for an extensive overview of what Net Nanny offers—https://www.netnanny.com/features/)

Qustodio -

- Filter Content and Apps - blocks inappropriate apps, games, and websites. Alerts you when they try to access blocked content.
- Monitors Activity
- Sets time limits
- GPS - Sends notifications when they arrive at home, school, or other destinations
- Tracks calls and SMS messages
- Detect suspicious contacts by seeing who your child exchanges calls and messages. Read the texts they send and receive, plus set a list of blocked phone numbers.

(Visit this site for an extensive overview of what Qustodio offers: https://www.qustodio.com/)

Other Parental Control Software Worth Mentioning:

mSpy - mSpy is one of the best parental control software for Android and iOS. It allows you to keep an eye on your child's phone activity remotely and is available globally. It notifies you of things like underage exposure, signs of bullying, pedophiles, etc. You can track internet use, locations, calls, social media usage, and block websites. It also gives you control over apps.

(Visit this site for an extensive overview of what MSpy monitors—https://www.mspy.com/)

Mobicip - Are you looking for versatile and powerful software to protect your kids on the dark web? Mobicip is listed on "Kids Safe" and can deliver on its promises. It is compatible with a variety of operating systems, one of the reasons it's one of our top picks. Features include monitoring, filtering, child data, privacy, locking, and inviting other users for reviews.

(Visit this site for an extensive overview of what Mobicip monitors—https://www.mobicip.com/)

Best Parental Controls for Gaming Consoles
The three video consoles are Xbox, PlayStation, and Nintendo Switch.

How to Set Parental Controls on Xbox - Xbox strives to create a place where everyone can play responsibly, within the boundaries they set, free from fear and intimidation. Xbox Series X|S, Xbox One, and Windows 10 devices come with unique family settings built in and created to help manage screen time, social interactions, online spending, and access to mature content, all from your phone and in real time. These URLs below will allow you to set up time limits, restrict access to adult content, control their ability to get on the internet, restrict purchases, and more:

https://www.xbox.com/en-US/community/for-everyone/responsible-gaming

https://support.microsoft.com/en-us/help/4028244/microsoft-account-set-up-screen-time-limits-for-your-child

https://www.xbox.com/en-US/xbox-one-s/family-entertainment

https://support.xbox.com/en-US/browse/xbox-one/security

https://support.xbox.com/en-US/xbox-one/security/core-family-safety-features

How to Set Parental Controls on PlayStation - Some of PlayStation's features are not free. These links will allow you to restrict access to adult content, control their ability to get on the internet, restrict purchases, control the ability to use it as a Blu-ray player, and more. You can also create time limits and time restrictions.

https://www.playstation.com/en-us/parental-controls/

https://www.playstation.com/en-gb/get-help/help-library/my-account/parental-controls/play-time-settings/

https://support.playstation.com/s/article/PS4-Parental-Controls?language=en_US

How to Set Parental Controls on Nintendo Switch - You can set limits on how long or how late the Nintendo Switch console can be used each day. When the time limit has been reached, an alarm notification will pop up on the screen. The app will also tell you if the Nintendo Switch console stays on past this time limit. If needed, you can always set the system to automatically interrupt the game when the time's up. Parents can disable play time alarms, and game suspension features temporarily or for a full day using their PIN.

https://www.nintendo.com/switch/parental-controls/

How to Limit the Time of Gaming on a Computer with Windows 10 -You can control access time on your child's computer using Windows 10 parental controls: https://kidlogger.net/blog/parental-control-in-windows-10.html

Other Parental Controls

How to Set Parental Controls on Amazon Prime - How to set up Restrictions on Prime Video on Web Prime Video restrictions allow you to limit the playback of content on Prime Video devices

https://www.amazon.com/gp/help/customer/display.html?
nodeId=201423060

How to Set Parental Controls on Google Play - How to turn on
parental controls to restrict what content can be downloaded or purchased from Google Play based on maturity level

https://support.google.com/googleplay/answer/1075738?hl=en

How to Set Parental Controls on Hulu - How to set up restrictions on PG-13, R- or Tv-MA content

https://www.cordcutters.com/how-use-parental-controls-hulu

How to Set Parental Controls on Netflix - To choose the types
of TV shows and movies your kids can watch, you can manage their
profiles individually or create a profile with the Netflix Kids experience
with titles just for kids.

https://help.netflix.com/en/node/264

How to Set Parental Controls on YouTube Kid - You can set up
separate profiles, restrict your child's experience to a more limited set of
videos by turning the Search feature off, block content based on age, or
approve content yourself (videos, channels, and collections that you've
handpicked grouped by topics, such as science and music)

https://support.google.com/youtubekids/answer/6172308?hl=en
(For regular YouTube, I have my child use my own account so that I
can view history and turn on safe search restrictions.)

Also, you can create trusted computers that bypass parental settings. It requires a little tech savvy, but through almost all routers
you can create a level of security, with most restriction abilities being
the same as Xfinity: https://www.cnet.com/how-to/how-to-use-your-
routers-parental-controls/

How to Set Parental Controls on Xfinity - Xfinity has built-in parental controls:

https://www.xfinity.com/support/articles/set-up-parental-controls-with-comcast-networking

RECOMMENDED RESOURCES

American Academy of Pediatrics - a valuable resource to create your personal family media plan to work for you and work within your family values and parenting style

https://www.healthychildren.org/English/media/Pages/default.aspx

Away for the Day—Stop Phone Use in Schools - Research shows that kids and teens do better with phones away during school hours. This movement is to get tools to parents, teachers, school leaders, and concerned individuals, so that you can go to your school and help institute policies where phones are put away.

https://www.awayfortheday.org/

Better Screen Time - focused on helping to create a tech-healthy family and teaching parents how to worry less and connect more. You'll find 100-plus screen-free ideas, excellent resources, and articles on how to have important conversations around screen time and create a family technology plan.

https://www.betterscreentime.com/

Center for Humane Technology - dedicated to radically reimagining our digital infrastructure. Their mission is to drive a comprehensive shift toward humane technology that supports families' well-being, democracy, and shared information environment.

https://www.humanetech.com/

Common Sense Media - reviews everything from apps and websites to movies, books, and television shows to help parents and teachers find the best content for children. The detailed reviews include aspects such as violence, language, and diversity.

https://www.commonsensemedia.org/

Cyberwise - a valuable resource site for busy grownups seeking to help youth use tech safely and wisely. They support, educate, and equip kids, educators, and families to build a healthy relationship with technology by providing research and tons of helpful information, videos, learning hubs, articles, and curriculum to teach at home on digital safety and online citizenship.

https://www.cyberwise.org/

The Digital Kids Initiative *focuses* on helping parents and educators become more aware of the technology children and teens use. It includes research-based articles and downloadable resources, including guides to sexting and cyberbullying.

https://digitalkidsinitiative.com/

Educate and Empower Kids - an organization made up of parents, professionals, and others devoted to the cause of empowering parents to create meaningful, long-lasting connection with their kids

https://educateempowerkids.org/about-us

Healthy Screen Habits – a non-profit organization that educates and empowers families to create healthy screen habits for screen use through raising awareness, providing tools, and creating change. They have all kinds of helpful tools and information to help you plan how to mindfully use technology and make wise choices in how you manage screen time.

https://www.healthyscreenhabits.org/tools

Screen-Free Week - supports families to take a break from screens on Saturdays, during family time, for a week in May, or anytime to play, explore, and rediscover the joys of life beyond ad-supported screens. During the first week of May, thousands of families, schools, and communities around the world will put down their entertainment screens for seven days of fun, connection, and discovery.

https://www.screenfree.org/

START - Stand Together and Rethink Technology - helps parents stand together and rethink technology—developing healthy norms, values, and training for tech use

https://www.westartnow.org/

Wait until 8th – a pledge that empowers parents to rally together to delay giving children a smartphone until at least the eighth grade. By banding together, this will decrease the pressure felt by kids and parents alike over the kids having a smartphone.

https://www.waituntil8th.org/

Movies to Watch to Encourage Conversations with Your Kids about Social Media

Selfless - The documentary *Selfless* opens conversation to the ever-growing epidemic of selfies, social media, and technology and how it is affecting us, body, mind, and soul. This story pushes away doom and gloom, offering a bright, beautiful film filled with messages of hope as we navigate this challenging time we live in.

Social Animals – an insightful documentary that looks at the pros and cons of Instagram

Social Dilemma – an eye-opening documentary about the effects and dangers of social media https://www.thesocialdilemma.com/

Promoting Positive Body Image

Confidence Kit: A Tool to Help Build Positive Body Confidence in Your Child - https://www.dove.com/us/en/dove-self-esteem-project/help-for-parents/confidence-kit-a-tool-to-help-build-positive-body-confidence.html

https://www.dove.com/us/en/dove-self-esteem-project/help-for-parents/confidence-kit-a-tool-to-help-build-positive-body-confidence.html

Websites by Topic

Cyberbullying

Cyberbullying Research Center - helping educators, parents, and youth work together to prevent and respond more effectively to cyberbullying, sexting, digital dating abuse, and related harms. Provides excellent downloadable resources for identifying, preventing, and responding to cyberbullying.

  https://cyberbullying.org/

Stop Bullying - provides information from various government agencies on what bullying is, what cyberbullying is, who is at risk, and how you can prevent and respond to bullying—a federal government website managed by the U.S. Department of Health and Human Services, helping educators, parents, and youth work together to prevent and respond more effectively to cyberbullying, sexting, digital dating abuse, and related harms

https://www.stopbullying.gov/

Pornography

Fight the New Drug - an interactive website that can help you have a conversation about porn with virtually anyone—including your kids

https://fightthenewdrug.org

How to Talk to Your Kids about Porn - all of the tips you need to navigate a conversation about porn successfully

https://fightthenewdrug.org/lets-talk-about-porn/

Culture Reframed - responding to the pornography crisis by providing education and support to promote healthy child and youth development

https://www.culturereframed.org/our-kids-online/

Defend Young Minds - geared towards younger kids, but they have excellent resources. They provide information, courses, and curriculum to educate, encourage and equip parents, professionals, and community leaders to empower young children with the information, skills, and mindsets they need to defend themselves against pornography and reject all forms of sexual exploitation.

https://www.defendyoungminds.com/

Fortify - a science-based recovery tool to help individuals quit pornography through comprehensive training, real-time analytics, and interactive support so that more people can find greater happiness and lasting love

https://www.joinfortify.com/

FAMILY CELL PHONE CONTRACT

Here are a few things I want to stress before you use this contract:

- I recommend you use this contract as a guide to enter into a discussion.
- Use it to fit your unique needs and the maturity of your child.
- Cross out what doesn't fit.
- Contracts work best particularly when your child has a say in the terms of the contract versus having the rules imposed upon him/her.
- Be flexible and remember to listen to your tween or teen's perspective.

You can access printable versions of our Cell Phone Contract here: https://momsoftweensandteens.com/cellphonecontract/

1. I understand that this phone is owned by my parents. The main reasons I am receiving this phone are: 1) to communicate with them, and 2) for personal safety.

2. All of my passwords and usernames for my phone, apps, and email will be known by my parents at all times. And, I will not be mad if they check my accounts.

3. Appropriate use times are __ a.m. - __ p.m. on weekdays and __a.m. - _ p.m. on weekends. At night my phone will be turned off and charged in an agreed-upon place.

4. I will not use the phone during homework, mealtimes, or any other time we agree upon.

5. I will not take videos or pictures of people without their permission. I will not use videos or photos of people because I think they're funny without permission.

6. I will never be mean or hurtful to someone in a text, post, or chat. I understand that once I hit "send," it is out in the world forever. Anyone can screenshot.

7. I will report bullying immediately.

8. I will never accept a friend request or chat request from someone I don't know in real life. I will never tell anyone where I live or post pictures of identifying places. I understand that someone who seems nice in a chat may not be who they say they are. The Stranger Danger rule applies here too.

9. I understand that I am responsible for losing or damaging my phone.

10. 11. I understand that this contract represents trust between my parents and me, and if I break that trust by violating any of these rules, there will be consequences, including, but not limited to, losing my phone privileges.

The following guidelines are for older kids:

11. I will not, under any circumstances, take photos of myself not fully clothed or of my private parts, or receive pictures of anyone else's private parts. This is illegal. I understand that any picture I take, or that someone else takes of me, can be screenshotted and shared with anyone in the world at any time.

12. The internet is full of inappropriate images and videos which can be accessed by mobile phones. If I am curious about these things, or have questions, I will ask my parents and not try to find them myself.

(Optional Note from Parents: *"Understand that the images you find online do not represent 'real life.' What your friends tell you 'they know' is not necessarily true and your phone is not the tool to find out—99 percent of the time your friends make stuff up to seem cool. We understand that it might be embarrassing to ask us. But we promise we will never joke or shy away from your questions, and we will give you the info you want."* ~ Love, Mom and/or Dad)

ACKNOWLEDGMENTS

First and foremost, thank you to my husband, Todd. You are the most supportive and encouraging husband I could ask for. Thank you for always having faith and believing in me. From the very beginning, you have invested in countless ways in my mission to serve and support moms of tweens and teens. You are the reason that we are where we are today. Without you, I could not have done it. I love you.

Thank you to my business partner, Jen Kehl. You are a gift from God that showed up at just the right time. How crazy is it that you are good at everything I am not? Thank you for making sense of all my workshop notes on technology, pulling all of my content together, and adding much-needed content based on your expertise. You are a blessing to me in more ways than I can count.

Thank you to Arlyn Lawrence, my gifted editor. You gave me the vision for what this book could be and have been incredibly positive and patient with me during this process. I am deeply grateful.

Thank you to my three beautiful kids, Sarah, Charley, and Lily. You are the joy of my life and you have each taught me so much. Without you, Moms of Tweens and Teens would not exist.

Thank you to all my personal clients and moms who have been a part of the Moms of Tweens and Teens Community. You are the reason I do what I do. I love your hearts. I love your desire to be the best moms and women you can be. Your steadfast love for your kids and your family inspires, encourages, and spurs me on daily. You are the reason I love what I do so very much. It is an incredible honor and privilege to be on this journey with you.

And finally, thank you to the team at Morgan James Publishing for their assistance and expertise in bringing this book to publication.

ABOUT THE AUTHOR

Sheryl Gould is a parenting expert and author who has been coaching moms for over 15 years. She is the founder of Moms of Tweens and Teens, an international organization supporting moms and helping them grow in their self-awareness, become more effective parents, and build stronger connections with their adolescents and families.

Sheryl loves supporting moms through her online community, local and online interactive workshops, Inner Circle membership, public speaking, and writing. Sheryl's mission for Moms of Tweens and Teens is to provide all moms a non-judgmental and compassionate place to share the struggles and triumphs of raising teens and tweens. She speaks to parents on a wide range of topics related to parenting adolescents, helping them to build healthier relationships and empowering their kids to thrive.

You can learn more, or connect with Sheryl, at www.momsoftweensandteens.com.

A free ebook edition is available with the purchase of this book.

To claim your free ebook edition:

1. Visit MorganJamesBOGO.com
2. Sign your name CLEARLY in the space
3. Complete the form and submit a photo of the entire copyright page
4. You or your friend can download the ebook to your preferred device

A **FREE** ebook edition is available for you or a friend with the purchase of this print book.

CLEARLY SIGN YOUR NAME ABOVE

Instructions to claim your free ebook edition:
1. Visit MorganJamesBOGO.com
2. Sign your name CLEARLY in the space above
3. Complete the form and submit a photo of this entire page
4. You or your friend can download the ebook to your preferred device

Print & Digital Together Forever.

Snap a photo

Free ebook

Read anywhere